A National Review of Scholastic Achievement in General Education
How Are We Doing and Why Should We Care?

by Steven J. Osterlind

ASHE-ERIC Higher Education Report Volume 25, Number 8

CALLAHAN LIBRARY
ST. JOSEPH'S COLLEGE
25 Audubon Avenue
Patchogue, NY 11772-2399

Prepared by

ERIC Clearinghouse on Higher Education
The George Washington University
URL: www.gwu.edu/~eriche

In cooperation with

Association for the Study
of Higher Education
URL: http://www.tiger.coe.missouri.edu/~ashe

Published by

Graduate School of Education and Human Development
The George Washington University
URL: www.gwu.edu

Jonathan D. Fife, Series Editor

Cite as
Osterlind, Steven J. 1997. *A National Review of Scholastic Achievement in General Education: How Are We Doing and Why Should We Care?* ASHE-ERIC Higher Education Report Volume 25, No. 8. Washington, D.C.: The George Washington University, Graduate School of Education and Human Development.

**Library of Congress Catalog Card Number
ISSN 0884-0040
ISBN 1-878380-80-y**

*Managing Editor: Lynne J. Scott
Manuscript Editor: Barbara Fishel/Editech
Cover Design by Michael David Brown, Inc., The Red Door Gallery, Rockport, ME*

The ERIC Clearinghouse on Higher Education invites individuals to submit proposals for writing monographs for the *ASHE-ERIC Higher Education Report* series. Proposals must include:
1. A detailed manuscript proposal of not more than five pages.
2. A chapter-by-chapter outline.
3. A 75-word summary to be used by several review committees for the initial screening and rating of each proposal.
4. A vita and a writing sample.

ERIC Clearinghouse on Higher Education
Graduate School of Education and Human Development
The George Washington University
One Dupont Circle, Suite 630
Washington, DC 20036-1183

> *The mission of the ERIC system is to improve American education by increasing and facilitating the use of educational research and information on practice in the activities of learning, teaching, educational decision making, and research, wherever and whenever these activities take place.*

This publication was prepared partially with funding from the Office of Educational Research and Improvement, U.S. Department of Education, under contract no. ED RR-93-002008. The opinions expressed in this report do not necessarily reflect the positions or policies of OERI or the Department.

EXECUTIVE SUMMARY

What Do We Really Know about Collegians' Scholastic Achievement?

Historically, the American public has accepted at face value the claims made by colleges and universities about the quality of postsecondary education (Pascarella and Terenzini 1991). Inquiry into their academic performance was unnecessary because scholastic rigor and excellence were tautologous. Recently, however, our conceptions of the postsecondary experience are changing, incorporating a more cynical and critical perspective. In consequence, a large number of colleges and universities have instituted assessment programs aimed at their core courses, their general education curricula, or their liberal studies programs.

Despite widespread use of outcomes assessment in American higher education, surprisingly little information is publicly available about what college students know and what skills they possess. The College Basic Academic Subjects Examination (College BASE), a first attempt to record nationally the achievement in general education for our college-level population, addresses this dearth of information about what collegians know and can do.

What Is College BASE, and Who Was Tested?

College BASE is a criterion-referenced achievement test focusing on the degree to which students have mastered particular skills and competencies consistent with the completion of general education coursework (Osterlind and Merz 1990). Used by 56 colleges and universities, it includes scores for 74,535 students tested between 1988 and 1993. This very large population of examinees makes College BASE perhaps the largest study of its kind ever. The sample of institutions and of students tested within any given campus was not random, but by convenience. Still, by size alone, this study represents a considerable number of students and institutions. Unlike other commercially available measures of general education outcomes, College BASE is, in fact, the only test for college-level audiences to meet the technical criteria for being "criterion-referenced." While approximately two-thirds of the items in College BASE assess high-level, cognitive reasoning skills, the remaining one-third of the items assess important, factual knowledge (Osterlind and Merz 1990).

College BASE assesses achievement in four subject areas: English, mathematics, science, and social studies. Subject-area scores are built on content "clusters," which in turn are based on "skills." For example, English scores are based on two content clusters: reading and literature, and writing. Mathematics scores are based on three clusters: general mathematics, algebra, and geometry. (Calculus is not included as another cluster, because it is not typically a part of a university's general education curriculum.) Cluster scores derive from the particular skills inherent to a given subject. For example, the cluster reading and literature comprises the skills of reading critically, reading analytically, and understanding literature. In total, the exam includes four subjects, nine clusters, and 23 skills.

In addition to examining test scores for the population of students generally, data were also analyzed by subpopulation along four categorical variables: sex, ethnic heritage, class standing, and age. Each variable has distinct features that divide it into meaningful units.

What Do Collegians Really Know about General Education Subjects?

The findings of the study suggest that wide differences exist in collegians' achievement in general education and that dissimilitude in achievement is especially pronounced for particular subpopulations, especially by race. Two main findings emerge from the first level of data interpretation, simple mean scores for the four subjects. First, scores in three of the four subject areas (mathematics, science, and social studies) are very close to each other and may be interpreted to mean that collegians' global level of achievement among these areas is about relatively equal. English, however, falls behind the other areas by several points, representing a truly significant difference.

Throughout all of the area tests, and regardless of whether one looks at data from the gross subject level or at the more detailed cluster and skill levels, the sexes differ in achievement. In English, for example, the data clearly show that females far outperform males. In the three other subjects, however—mathematics, science, and social studies—males evidently demonstrate superior knowledge over females. And this trend seems to carry forward into analysis by cluster and skill level.

Interethnic differences are not consistent. For example, enormous disparity exists within the Asian population between achievement in mathematics and achievement in the three other subjects, especially when contrasted to English. Within the Hispanic subpopulation, social studies scores are significantly stronger than scores in the other areas. Achievement across subjects is more uniform for Caucasians than it is for any other ethnic heritage classification, and it is most dissimilar for Asians/Pacific Islanders.

Most alarming, however, are the findings between and among the race groupings. In this area, differences are profound and pronounced. In mathematics, Asian students outperform all other groups, whereas Caucasians' achievement outstrips all other groups in English, science, and social studies. Blacks/African Americans lag far behind the achievement of all other ethnic heritage groups in every area assessed. In some cases, the gap between Blacks'/African Americans' achievement and the other groups is so wide it is more than just alarming. It is frightening.

What Are the Implications of College BASE? What Further Research Is Called For?

The implications of the findings from this study are many and varied, and include the necessity for special programs for low-achieving students and more opportunities to extend the collegiate experience for high achievers. Mostly, however, the findings show the vast differences within the population of college students. The full report contains considerable discussion about the significance and implications of the study's findings.

At this point in our history of higher education, it would be worthwhile to systematically sample the achievement of students who are pursuing formal postsecondary education in a nationally based research project. These findings and their interpretations show that achievement in general education among collegians is a complex and intriguing arena for exploration. Findings and conclusions are at once disturbing and enlightening. But at least by a national look at the achievement of college-level students in general education, we begin to gain insight into evaluating the quality and effectiveness of American higher education.

CONTENTS

Foreword	xi
Introduction	**1**
Description of This Study	5
What Is General Education?	6
The College BASE Instrument	**11**
Test Content	14
Calibration and Scoring	18
Evidence of Reliability and Validity	23
The Students	25
The Colleges and Universities	25
The Study Variables	27
A Call for a National Study	28
The Findings	**31**
Global Findings	31
Findings for English Subject	46
Differences in English Achievement by Sex	52
Differences in English Achievement by Ethnic Heritage	53
Differences in English Achievement by Class Standing	57
Differences in English Achievement by Age	58
Findings for Mathematics Subject	59
Differences in Mathematics Achievement by Sex	63
Differences in Mathematics Achievement by Ethnic Heritage	64
Differences in Mathematics Achievement by Class Standing	66
Differences in Mathematics Achievement by Age	67
Findings for Science Subject	68
Differences in Science Achievement by Sex	70
Differences in Science Achievement by Ethnic Heritage	71
Differences in Science Achievement by Class Standing	74
Differences in Science Achievement by Age	74
Findings for Social Studies Subject	74
Differences in Social Studies Achievement by Sex	77
Differences in Social Studies Achievement by Ethnic Heritage	77
Differences in Social Studies Achievement by Class Standing	78
Differences in Social Studies Achievement by Age	78

Concluding Discussion	**81**
Tables	
1. Classifications and Numbers of Examinees within Categorical Variables	26
2. Ranked Mean Scaled Scores for General Education Subjects	33
3. Ranked Mean Scaled Scores for General Education Clusters	36
4. Percent of Students in Each Mastery Classification for General Education Skills	38
5. Ranking by Percent of Students in Each Mastery Classification for General Education Skills	39
6. Mean Scaled Scores for Subjects by Classificatory Variable Sex	40
7. Mean Scaled Scores for Subjects by Classificatory Variable Ethnic Heritage	41
8. Mean Scaled Scores for Subjects by Classificatory Variable Class Standing	43
9. Mean Scaled Scores for Subjects by Classificatory Variable Age	44
10. Mean p-Value of Test Items for Population and by Classificatory Variable	45
11. English Subject and Cluster Mean Scaled Scores for Total Population and by Classificatory Variable	48
12. Math Subject and Cluster Mean Scaled Scores for Total Population and by Classificatory Variable	60
13. Science Subject and Cluster Mean Scaled Scores for Total Population and by Classificatory Variable	69
14. Social Studies Subject and Cluster Mean Scaled Scores for Total Population and by Classificatory Variable	76
Figures	
1. Two Frequency Distributions Comparing Group Achievement	14
2. Outline of Content for College BASE	16
3. Hierarchical Design of the Exam	18
4. Item Used to Assess the Skill of Analytical Reading	19
5. Item Used to Assess a Basic Geometric Skill	20
6. Item Used to Assess the Skill of Recognizing Principal Elements in an Experiment	21
7. Item Used to Assess the Skill of Recognizing the Significance of World Events	22

8. Relative Differences in Scaled Scores for the Four Subjects	33
9. Relative Differences in Scaled Scores for Subjects between Males and Females	40
10. Relative Differences in Scaled Scores for Subjects among Ethnic Heritage Categories	42
11. Relative Differences in Scaled Scores for Subjects among Class Standing Categories	43
12. Relative Differences in Scaled Scores for Subjects among Age Categories	44
13. Item Used to Assess a Reason-based Skill in General Mathematics	62
14. Item Used to Assess the Skill of Interpreting and Expressing Results in Science	73
15. Item Used to Assess the Skill of Recognizing the Significance of World Political and Economic Structures in Social Studies	79
References	**89**
Index	**95**
ASHE-ERIC Higher Education Reports	**105**
Advisory Board	107
Consulting Editors	109
Review Panel	111
Recent Titles	115
Order Form	

FOREWORD

Efforts to foster quality and excellence in higher education and to link quality performance with an institution's educational mission have moved from curiosity about innovation to the early phase of implementation. Linking performance with outcomes continues to be emphasized. The theme of the 1997 annual meeting of the Middle States Association of Colleges and Schools, for example, was "accreditation and quality assurance," while that for the 1998 annual meeting of the National Education Association is "on the cutting edge of quality: the power of collective action in higher education." President Clinton included in his 1998 budget for the U.S. Department of Commerce funds to recognize excellence in education through the annual Malcolm Baldrige National Quality Awards, and although Congress did not appropriate these funds, the National Institute for Standards and Technology has developed educational criteria in anticipation that such awards will be approved in future budgets. The August 15, 1997, issue of the *Chronicle of Higher Education* (p. A23) reported that, in a survey of state higher education officials, "more than half of the states expect to have embraced the idea of holding public colleges financially accountable for their performance. . . ."

This interest in linking performance and outcomes is more than just a passing fancy. It is a significant change in society's fundamental belief about education. Educators' old philosophy that "you cannot measure what we value" is giving way to a public philosophy that "if you are not measuring it, you do not value it." Concurrently, a belief among faculty that "if we do our best, we have quality" is giving way to a value that "it's not quality unless it supports the educational mission of the institution." This value recognizes the interrelationship and interdependency of programs within an institution and between curricular areas.

This report by Steven J. Osterlind, professor of educational psychology in the College of Education and director of graduate studies at the University of Missouri–Columbia, analyzes the academic achievement of students in general education courses. It is more than just an academic exercise examining the state of the art of general education. The author carefully examines differences in four specific subject areas (English, mathematics, science, and social studies) and in academic achievement by sex, ethnic heritage, class standing, and age. As the author notes, the "findings and conclusions are at once disturbing and enlightening."

This report provides not only insight into the national picture of the quality of American higher education, but also direction for individual institutions as they begin to examine their own effectiveness. Institutions and their faculty must become part of the process of helping to define the standards and direct the process that will produce the excellence to help achieve their institutions' educational missions. But it cannot be done without knowing quantitatively and qualitatively what the current academic achievement is within their institutions. Institutional leaders who take time to assess current academic achievement, working as partners with their faculty, will be better able to develop sound strategies for achieving higher levels of academic excellence.

Jonathan D. Fife
Series Editor,
Professor of Higher Education Administration, and
Director, ERIC Clearinghouse on Higher Education

INTRODUCTION

Historically, the American public has accepted at face value the claims made by colleges and universities about the quality of postsecondary education (Pascarella and Terenzini 1991). Inquiry into their academic performance was not necessary because scholastic rigor and excellence were tautologous. They are, after all, in the public's mind places of *higher* learning and repositories of new knowledge. It is a historical American truth that sending a son or daughter to college represents a kind of "success meter" for parents. And if the collegian is the first person in a family to pursue education beyond high school, the accomplishment is thought to be still sweeter.

Examining the quality of colleges' and universities' educational offerings has not been part of the national conversation. We like our colleges. They are places to be valued and, in former times, even revered. Our image of colleges and universities was firmly fixed in the warm psychology of good thoughts.

Recently, however, our conceptions of the postsecondary experience have begun to change, incorporating a more cynical and critical perspective. The new viewpoint on colleges and universities is not the same us-versus-them outlook that dominated the public's perceptions of campus activities during the antiwar period of the late 1960s and early 1970s; instead, we take a more practical approach to looking at the college experience, often focusing on whether it will lead to a job and how much it costs. The tenor of these questions is a growing disaffection with the value of the campus experience.

Reflecting the public's disaffection, articles and scholarly papers questioning the value of a college education began appearing with increasing frequency in both the academic and popular presses (Grossman 1988; Hartle 1985). The National Institute of Education's *A Nation at Risk* (National Commission 1983) typified this general disenchantment with American education in general in a statement that reverberated across America:

> *If an unfriendly foreign power had attempted to impose on America the mediocre educational performance that exists today, we might well have viewed it as an act of war* (p. 5).

Although the authors of this remarkable statement directed their distress at elementary and secondary schools, the national perturbation spilled over to postsecondary education. Several blue-ribbon advisory panels focused specifically on higher education. The Study Group on the Conditions of Excellence in American Higher Education (1984), the Association of American Colleges (1985), the Southern Regional Education Board (1985), the National Governors Association (1986), the Carnegie Foundation for the Advancement of Teaching (see Boyer 1987), and, most recently, the Wingspread Group (1993) all issued reports criticizing the quality of higher education and calling upon colleges and universities to assess students' progress toward institutional objectives.

The Wingspread Group's report is "an open letter to those concerned about the American future," and it seems to capture the current mood and tone of the public's attitude toward higher education. It says simply, "Education is in trouble and with it our nation's hope for the future" (Wingspread Group 1993, p. 1). The report goes on to issue several challenges to the higher education community to improve markedly the intellectual capital of its product, that is, the students. The spirit of those challenges is summed up in its conclusion:

> *A generation ago, we told educators we wanted more people with a college credential and more research-based knowledge. Educators responded accordingly. Now we need to ask for different things. Students must value* achievement, *not simply seek a credential* (Wingspread Group 1993, p. 24).

Certainly, our image of colleges and universities has changed immeasurably. No longer do we believe in congenital goodness for postsecondary education. Colleges and universities now have their share of angst riders.

In response to the public's growing antipathy toward many colleges and universities, the federal government, several states, and some accrediting associations have begun urging, and in some instances even requiring, that postsecondary institutions assess the educational outcomes of students to document and improve the quality and effectiveness of their academic programs (Ewell 1991). Institutions have heeded the call in vast numbers. The most recent *Campus Trends* survey (El-Khawas 1990) found that 82 percent of America's colleges and universities had implemented, or were implementing, outcomes assessment.

Moreover, because a focal point of many of the criticisms aimed at the core work of most colleges and universities—that is, their general education or liberal studies programs—these new efforts at assessment tended to examine the quality of institutions' general education programs (Centra 1988; Pike 1992a). Among campuses with existing comprehensive student assessment programs, 67 percent have programs to evaluate this core ingredient of the college experience (Johnson, Prus, Andersen, and El-Khawas 1991).

Despite widespread use of outcomes assessment in American higher education, surprisingly little information is publicly available about what college students know and what skills they possess. An exhaustive review of 20 years of research into how college affects students concludes that:

> ... *the body of evidence concerning the net effects of college on the development and general cognitive skills is small and limited in scope* (Pascarella and Terenzini 1991, p. 155).

This regrettable conclusion was corroborated by the Resource Group on Adult Literacy and Lifelong Learning, which noted in its interim report to the National Education Goals Panel (1991) that neither national nor state information is currently available on the ability of college graduates to "think critically, communicate effectively, and solve problems" (p. 95). And the dearth of information about the level of collegians' academic attainments is regrettable.

Not only is little known about whether the college experience helps to develop young minds. Public cynicism about its value is reinforced when we read, as we did in *U.S. News & World Report*'s influential guide "Best College Rankings" (*"U.S. News"* 1995), that some schools, in an effort to make their programs more attractive to prospective students, omitted from their reporting students with low test scores or other undesirable characteristics, such as academic probation.

While it is true that few research studies or reports have been done on the achievement of postsecondary students and that no national database exists on postsecondary education outcomes, it does not follow that we know nothing about the knowledge and skills of college students. Four tests of the outcomes of postsecondary general education have been widely used since 1987 (Pike 1989). Additionally, an enormous body of information covers collegians on a variety of subjects related to achievement, including grade point averages, graduated rates, and SAT and GRE scores. And nontrivial, anecdotal evidence abounds about collegians' scholastic attainments. Individually as well as collectively, these indicators contribute to our understanding of what collegians know and can do.

There is also an entire realm of achievement tests used only in postsecondary institutions for assessing students. Some contend that achievement testing at this level was actually ushered in by the introduction of the GRE's area tests in 1954 (Pace 1979). Moreover, three earlier landmark studies attempted to assess students' scholastic achievement during their college careers, including the Pennsylvania Study, the Cooperative Study in General Education, and the Cooperative Study of Evaluation in General Education (Pace 1979). But neither the advent of the GRE nor the summative historical reviews of the assessment movement (Pace 1984; Sims 1992) took into account skill-based, criterion-referenced measurement of collegians' academic achievement nationally, across many campuses.

If, however, one looks to campus assessment generally, often to the exclusion of hard data on scholastic achievement, an impressive body of relevant literature exists. One search of relevant databases yielded over 300 studies on campus assessment since 1980 alone. Annual conferences are devoted to the topic. Regrettably, and commonly, the literature on campus assessment specifically excludes indicators of data on students' achievement. Instead, many studies refer to satisfaction surveys, interviews, and the allocation of resources as the complete data source for institutional assessment.

Another striking feature of the research and information that is known about campus assessment is its idiosyncratic nature. A scan of research titles and journal abstracts tells one promptly that the reported information is about *just* a specific program or effort on a particular campus. The expense and complexity of conducting multicampus assessments is obviously a formidable task for most researchers.

Thus, one can reach a number of conclusions about the state of campus assessment at many colleges and universities:

1. It is common for campuses to have planned for and installed an assessment program.

2. Nearly all of the research done on assessment programs is delimited to just a single campus.
3. The studies of campus assessment frequently exclude data on students' achievement.
4. Few standardized tests are available nationally for collecting data on this group of students' achievement.
5. Psychometrically based national norms on postsecondary students' achievement have never been developed.

Description of This Study

This study seeks to address the dearth of broadly generalizable information on collegians' scholastic learning by reporting eight years of experience with one of the nationally used measures of postsecondary general education, the College Basic Academic Subjects Examination (College BASE) (Osterlind et al. 1988–1995). The study itself includes more than 73,000 students who attended one of more than 56 colleges and universities. This very large population of examinees makes this study of collegians' achievement perhaps the largest study of its kind to date. (While an enormous body of achievement-related research uses the GRE or one of the popular college admissions tests [e.g., ACT, SAT], it cannot be considered in the same category of testing as College BASE, for those tests are neither true achievement tests [they are akin to quasi–ability measures] nor designed to assess scholastic attainment derived from the college experience.)

It is important to note from the outset that the test results reported here do not provide a nationally representative profile of college students' knowledge and skills, at least in the exact sense prescribed by statistical sampling. In fact, a statistically verifiable national study of collegians' achievement *should* be conducted. (We later outline a few considerations for undertaking such a huge task.) Nonetheless, the results of the present study do provide a starting point for evaluating the quality and effectiveness of American higher education. After all (as described later), the test instrument is very strong and includes more than 73,000 individuals from a large number of diverse institutions. What can be gleaned from this investigation is that scholastic achievement in general education across this vast array of differences can speak loudly about what collegians know generally.

The results also suggest that the picture may not be as bleak as presented by *A Nation at Risk,* the popular press, and the reports of national advisory panels, although some serious deficiencies exist in academic achievement, especially for particular subgroups of collegians. The picture is actually quite complex. At the least, this study is a first attempt to capture information on the general educational attainments of college students nationally.

The uniqueness of this study is at once surprising and startling. It is surprising because it presents a first attempt to capture nationwide data about the general educational achievement of a college-level population. Although nationwide testing of achievement, ability, and aptitude is common, even habitual, for elementary and secondary school children, it had never been attempted on a nationwide scale with a postsecondary population until this study using College BASE.

And the study is startling because of its findings. Huge differences exist among collegians' achievement in the skills associated with general education, and vast discrepancies are evident in the skills among particular subpopulations of collegians, specifically, sex, ethnic heritage, class standing, and age.

What Is General Education?
When discussing collegians' achievement, whether in this study or in more general discussions of postsecondary achievement, it is important to be aware of what colleges and universities consider "general education." As a term, "general education" has no generic meaning and can only be made sensible in the context of looking at what a particular school requires as core coursework for its students. There are huge differences among schools about what constitutes general education (Katz 1995). For example, consider Stanford University in Palo Alto, California, often cited as one of the world's truly great universities. At Stanford, general education includes a broad range of courses with a decidedly political focus. Students must pass a civilization course in which non-Western, ethnocentric shibboleths are the primary focus, and they must enroll in many such courses.

In contrast, just up the road from Stanford, in Marin County, stands Thomas Aquinas University. While scarcely a Stanford in name recognition, the academic rigor of this college's general education requirement far surpasses that of its southern neighbor. At Thomas Aquinas, all students are trained in classical education by reading the original works of literally hundreds of time-tested thinkers, including Plato, Chaucer, Goethe, Marx, Milton, Descartes, Cromwell, Boswell, and Shakespeare. There can scarcely be a more bipolar example of the intent for "general education" than the comparison of Stanford and Thomas Aquinas, and these two places point out the huge differences that exist in general education.

A rough parallel to this wide-ranging debate about what constitutes general education is psychologists' use of the word "intelligence." In psychology, no uniform definition of intelligence exists. Some psychologists characterize it behaviorally, while others look at intelligence cognitively. The words these differing psychologists use to describe intelligence are as far apart as Stanford's and Thomas Aquinas's requirements for general education. Still, understanding intelligence, however phrased, is important to all sides, and measuring it can be accomplished with remarkable reliability—which leads us to understand the importance and high significance of assessing general education across many universities. It is not to deny vast differences; rather, it is to know the common ground.

Despite the vast differences in general education course requirements across universities, there are many commonalities. The Lilly Foundation's Project on Strong Foundations for General Education (1994) identified 12 principles that constitute an effective general education program. A decidedly strong emphasis among the principles is an institution's steady focus on strong academics.

These studies, and others, consistently document that students' admission to even be eligible to undergo a course of study in general education changed dramatically with the advent of intellectual relativism in the 1970s and before. It is well worth the time to consider the admission requirements to Harvard University in 1892, before general education. This citation from Harvard's admission handbook, given to prospective candidates, makes the point.

> *The studies required for admission are divided into two classes, elementary and advanced. The first class is prescribed for all students except under two conditions, which will be mentioned later, while the second class is elective. Without going into troublesome details, it may be said that the examinations in the elementary studies test the following acquirements: an elementary working*

knowledge of four languages, two ancient, Latin and Greek, and two modern, French and German; some acquaintance with English classical literature, and the ability to write clearly and intelligently about the books [that] have been read; a knowledge of elementary algebra and plane geometry; an acquaintance with the laws and phenomena of physics obtained from experiments performed by the pupil in a laboratory, or a knowledge of descriptive physics and elementary astronomy; and last, a knowledge of the history and geography either of ancient Greece and Rome or modern England and America. In addition to examinations in these prescribed elementary studies, the candidate must be examined on two more subjects, chosen, according to his tastes and natural aptitude, from the following list of nine advanced studies: Latin translation, Greek translation, Latin and Greek composition, French, German, trigonometry and solid geometry or trigonometry and analytical geometry, advanced algebra and analytical geometry, physics, chemistry (Greenough 1892, p. 671).

That admission requirements—and along with them institutions' concepts of general education—have changed in dramatic and remarkable ways can scarcely be made more evident than comparing Harvard's 100-year-old admission requirements with those of today at many universities, including Harvard. An admissions officer at Harvard has said that they do not use any standard test scores in their judgments; rather, they look at the "whole of life experiences" and form a more "generalistic" opinion. While a candidate's class rank may be important, it may be outweighed by his or her involvement in community service projects. The prescriptive content of the old requirements for admission is nowhere to be found in today's version.

New concepts of general education are currently being offered. Some think, for example, that a general education curriculum should include character-building elements and should "involve acquiring four arts of character (sensitivity, originality, engagement, and commitment) that merge the different modes of thought into the common enterprise of good general education" (Kaplan 1995, p. 359). Others advocate having different general education requirements for older students as they become an increasingly larger segment of the overall student body (Giczkowski 1995) or using a spiritual approach to define general education as the best way to bring about transmission of transcendent truths in general education (McWilliams 1993). The literature is replete with other approaches and suggestions for an evolving general education.

From this brief discussion, then, one can see the importance of being ever mindful of the vastly different and ever-changing notion of what constitutes general education in contemporary American colleges and universities.

THE COLLEGE BASE INSTRUMENT

This section takes a look at the College Basic Academic Subjects Examination (Osterlind et al. 1988–1995), the instrument from which the data in the study derive, to help understand the precise nature of what has been assessed. The focus is on identifying the kinds of errors in measurement that occur and how much error exists in the instrument. Knowing the amount of error in the instrument is critical to understanding the importance of the findings yielded by a measure of mental ability.

College BASE is a criterion-referenced achievement test that focuses on the degree to which students have mastered particular skills and competencies consistent with the completion of general education coursework (Osterlind and Merz 1990). Unlike other commercially available measures of general education outcomes, such as the Academic Profile (Educational Testing Service 1989), College Outcome Measures Program (American College Testing 1986), and Collegiate Assessment of Academic Proficiency (American College Testing 1989), College BASE is a criterion-referenced test of achievement in collegiate-level general education. It has no other stated purpose. In fact, of the tests mentioned, it is the only one to meet technical criteria for having the appellation "criterion-referenced." Such criteria speak to issues involved in developing the goals and aims for a test, in deriving particular methods for constructing a test, and in interpreting the scores yielded by a test.

It is a common misnomer to call a test "criterion-referenced" merely because it has objectives. And, as more and more test makers are wont to do, it is an another common misnomer to call a test both CRT and NRT, that is, criterion-referenced and norm-referenced. A CRT (criterion-referenced test) may yield normed information, but not vice versa. Quality of the interpretation of the test's scores, that is to say, validity, is the cause of these frequent misunderstandings. College BASE, on the other hand, meets technical criteria of a true CRT.

By virtue of the fact that it is a true criterion-referenced instrument, both absolute and relative scores on College BASE can be used to assess students' knowledge and skills and to evaluate the quality and effectiveness of academic programs (Pike 1992a). College BASE also differs from other commercially available national general education tests in that it contains some items designed specifically to measure students' recall of factual information. While approximately two-thirds of the items in College BASE assess high-level, cognitive reasoning skills, the remaining one-third assess important, factual knowledge (Osterlind and Merz 1990).

Because critics of tests often cite "factual recall" as evidence for arguments against testing, it may be useful to explain what is involved in knowing facts. Simply put, it is the stuff of knowledge and involves comprehension, analysis, synthesis, and evaluation. Memory (a much maligned but basic skill in all human experience), too, is an important ingredient in factual recall. Factual knowledge employs all the cognitive skills.

But, just as important, factual knowledge as presumed for College BASE is not presumed to be just anything that can be known or labeled a noun. In College BASE, factual knowledge refers to fundamental bits of information that form the very bricks of the knowledge edifice. For example, knowing three times four equals twelve is a fact, but it is not true "factual knowledge" as the term is used in College BASE. Instead, knowing *how* to multiply two numbers (whether two and two or sixteen and six) is factual knowledge.

Another example of factual knowledge in College BASE can be seen in the historical facts needed for answers. The precise year of the Yalta Conference is an important fact, but it too does not qualify for College BASE's factual knowledge because it is too idiosyncratic. On the other hand, knowing whether the Yalta Conference took place at the beginning of the war (and which war) or at the end is significant factual recall and qualifies to appear on College BASE. The reason stems from its significance in world affairs for the next 50 years of history. The specific calendar year is not what gives the conference its significance; rather, its import derives from its relationship to World War II. Thus, a factual recall item about the Yalta Conference on College BASE would not ask what particular year the conference occurred; it would ask whether the conference took place before or after the war. From this example, it can be seen that including a specific bit of information as a factual recall item on College BASE is done with great care and for a given purpose.

At this point, it may also be useful to describe the word "relative" from a technical perspective, because it is used liberally throughout the study. In measurement, "relative" refers to a given comparison between two or more subjects in a specialized way. To say that one subject is relatively higher than another is not to suggest a direct or absolute comparison between them. Nowhere does the study directly contrast two distinct subjects (e.g., reading and mathematics), because they are, after all, different. Instead, they are compared in a different and more accurate way. Each subject is set against a standard called the "norming population," and the higher an individual is in comparison with the norming population, the greater the achievement in that subject. When two subjects are contrasted, then, and one is higher in comparison to the norm group for that subject than he or she is in comparison to the norm group for the other subject, then the individual is "relatively" higher.

An example may clarify the point. Suppose you are studying two foreign languages simultaneously, say, French and German. Some of your peers are also learning French to a certain degree, and others are learning German to a certain degree. At some point, your achievement in both subjects is assessed, and you are found to be above the peer group in German but below the other peer group in French. This result does not suggest that French is directly compared with German; rather, it shows that your achievement in German is "relatively" stronger than it is in French. Hence, throughout this report with regard to contrasting subjects, "relative" is used in this technical sense.

Another important point to bear in mind when considering the study's findings is that all of the data and hence the interpretive comments in this report are based on aggregate data or test scores that are derived from very large groups of examinees. Most of the scores discussed are simple mean scores or standard deviations. In the few instances in which mean scores are not used, the statistic employed is described. Reporting and interpreting aggregate, mean scores can be quite useful, but it also carries the possibility of misinterpretation. Mean scores do not reflect the range of scores obtained by the population, and, an important point, they do not reflect any given individual. This last point is so significant that it warrants further discussion.

Mean scores are simply a convenient way to describe a lot of individual scores, but in doing so they misrepresent any particular score. It is a bit like saying that the mean number of children is 2.3 for the typical American family; obviously, no family has 2.3 children! Hence, the statement misdescribes the individual, and the phenomenon is termed the "law of the individual." It is an important point to bear in mind when reading this report.

Further, the law of the individual reminds us to be sensitive to people and to avoid stereotyping them by incorrectly imagining that all individuals in a group have the achievement represented by the simple mean score. The big picture should not override the importance of the individual accomplishment. Of course, a range of scores occurs for any group, and often it is quite large, showing that many individuals are very low and very high. If we say, for example, that one group is half a standard deviation above another group, it belies the fact that there are many individuals in the lower-achieving group that actually outperformed some individuals in the higher-achieving group.

Figure 1 displays this phenomenon graphically. The shaded area indicates the persons in the lower-achieving group who outperformed many in the higher-achieving group. This law of the individual reminds us to avoid stereotyping and to treat each person with the respect for individual differences that make us unique. This report maintains such respect.

Test Content
The objectives assessed by College BASE stem from the summary report of the College Entrance Examination Board's

FIGURE 1

Two Frequency Distributions Comparing Group Achievement

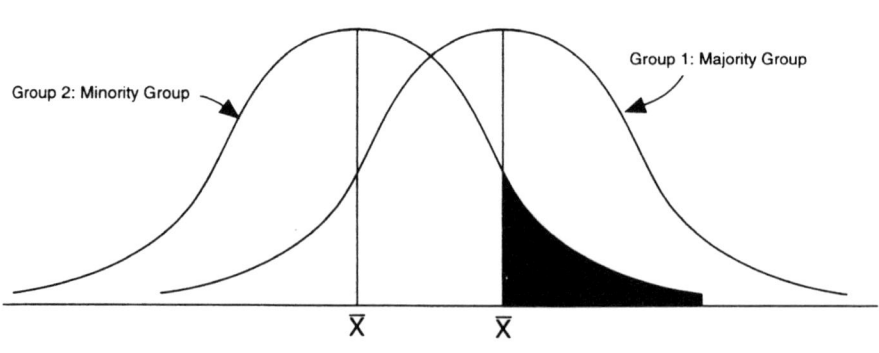

Educational EQuality Project, *Educational EQuality. Academic Preparation for College: What Students Need to Know and Be Able to Do* (1983). According to its authors, the knowledge and skills outlined in the report represent learned competencies that are developed through education and practice. The outcomes for learners identified by the project offer a carefully developed breadth of coverage for particular subjects that incorporates the important components of topics but does not include trivial or idiosyncratic issues.

Using the College Board report as a starting point, the test's author at the Center for Educational Assessment of the University of Missouri–Columbia embarked on an 18-month project to identify outcomes for learners in general education. For this effort, the test author enlisted the aid of persons from colleges and universities throughout the country with expertise in specific curricular areas. A list of potential names was developed by requesting nationally recognized subject-related organizations, such as national councils of teachers of English, mathematics, science, and social studies, and the Association for Supervision and Curriculum Development, to submit nominations. Additional names were added to the list based on reputation or other recommendations. In all, over 100 persons representing more than 50 institutions of higher education from 20 states were identified and included on the advisory panel (Osterlind and Merz 1990).

Through meetings and rounds of review by mail and telephone, advisory panel members reacted to the original list of outcomes for learners and developed them into a four-tiered schema, including subjects, clusters, skills, and enabling subskills. Additionally, a set of competencies was derived representing a curriculum common to most institutions of higher learning (Osterlind and Merz 1990). As suggestions were received, they were reviewed, discussed, and then incorporated into subsequent drafts of the test's content. This schema became the test's organizational framework.

College BASE assesses achievement in four "subject" areas: English, mathematics, science, and social studies. Subject-area scores are built on content "clusters," which in turn are based on "skills." For example, English scores are based on two content clusters: reading and writing. Mathematics subject scores are based on three clusters: general mathematics, algebra, and geometry. (Calculus is not included in the exam as another cluster, because it is not typically part of a university's general education curriculum.) Cluster scores derive from the particular skills inherent to a given subject. For example, the cluster "reading and literature" comprises the skills of reading critically, reading analytically, and understanding literature. In total, the exam includes four subjects, nine clusters, and 23 skills. Figure 2 depicts the hierarchical structure of College BASE's content.

FIGURE 2
Outline of Content for College BASE

College BASE Subjects, Clusters and Skills

ENGLISH

Clusters	Skills
Reading & Literature	Read accurately and critically by asking pertinent questions about a text, by recognizing assumptions and implications, and by evaluating ideas.
	Read a literary text analytically, seeing relationships between form and content.
	Understand a range of literature, rich in quality and representative of different literary forms and historical contexts.
Writing	Understand the various elements of the writing process, including collecting information and formulating ideas, determining relationships, arranging sentences and paragraphs, establishing transitions, and revising what has been written.
	Use the conventions of standard written English.
	Write an organized, coherent, and effective essay.

MATHEMATICS

Clusters	Skills
General Mathematics Proficiency	Use mathematical techniques in the solution of real-life problems.
	Use the language, notation, and deductive nature of mathematics to express quantitative ideas with precision.
	Use the techniques of statistical reasoning and recognize common misuses of statistics.
Algebra	Evaluate algebraic and numerical expressions.
	Solve equations and inequalities.
Geometry	Recognize two- and three-dimensional figures and their properties.
	Use the properties of two- and three-dimensional figures to perform geometrical calculations.

SCIENCE

Clusters	Skills
Laboratory & Field Work	Recognize the role of observation and experimentation in the development of scientific theories.
	Recognize appropriate procedures for gathering scientific information through laboratory and field work.
	Interpret and express results of observation and experimentation.
Fundamental Concepts	Understand the fundamental concepts, principles, and theories of the life sciences.
	Understand the fundamental concepts, principles, and theories of the physical sciences.

SOCIAL STUDIES

Clusters	Skills
History	Recognize the chronology and significance of major events and movements in world history.
	Recognize the chronology and significance of major events and movements in United States history.
Social Sciences	Recognize basic features and concepts of world geography.
	Recognize basic features and concepts of the world's political and economic structures.
	Recognize appropriate investigative and interpretive procedures in the social sciences.

Not shown in figure 2 are the "enabling subskills" that underlie the skills. Enabling subskills provide explicit descriptions of a given skill's constituent parts. During the exam's development, they are particularly useful in that they furnish precise instructions to writers of the test's items, helping to ensure the proper breadth of coverage. For example, the enabling subskills of the skill "reading accurately and critically" are (1) ascertaining the meaning of a passage, identifying main ideas, supporting details, and logical or narrative sequences; (2) recognizing the implicit assumptions and values underlying a written work; and (3) evaluating the ideas presented in a text by determining their logical validity, their implications, and their relationships to ideas beyond the text (Osterlind and Merz 1990). Item writers used these enabling skills as a guide in constructing test items intended to reflect a given content. Most of the skills have three or four enabling subskills, summing to a total of 73 enabling subskills for the exam.

In addition to content knowledge, College BASE assesses three "reasoning competencies" across disciplines: interpretive reasoning, strategic reasoning, and adaptive reasoning. The model underlying these cognitive-processing competencies is based on the work of Hannah and Michaelis (1977). The model assumes factual recall as foundational to higher-level reasoning. According to the model, interpretive reasoning is the most basic level of information processing beyond factual recall; it includes such abilities as paraphrasing, summarizing, and explaining. The next level of information processing, strategic reasoning, includes skills related to definition, comparison, and classification. Adaptive reasoning includes abilities such as synthesis and evaluation. The reasoning competencies are integrated with the hierarchical subject-cluster-skill design to form a content/cognitive process matrix for the exam (see figure 3). The essential point for the matrix is to prepare a strong foundation for the interpretation of test scores based on relevant general education content with appropriate reasoning skills.

Figures 4, 5, 6, and 7 present one illustration from each subject area. Some of the findings discussed in later sections of this report refer to these items, which are presented to give the reader a sense of the kinds of questions included in College BASE. They are all in multiple-choice format, but they do not require just simple recall of factual information. More often, the items call upon an examinee to synthesize, judge, or evaluate some information before responding.

FIGURE 3
Hierarchical Design of the Exam

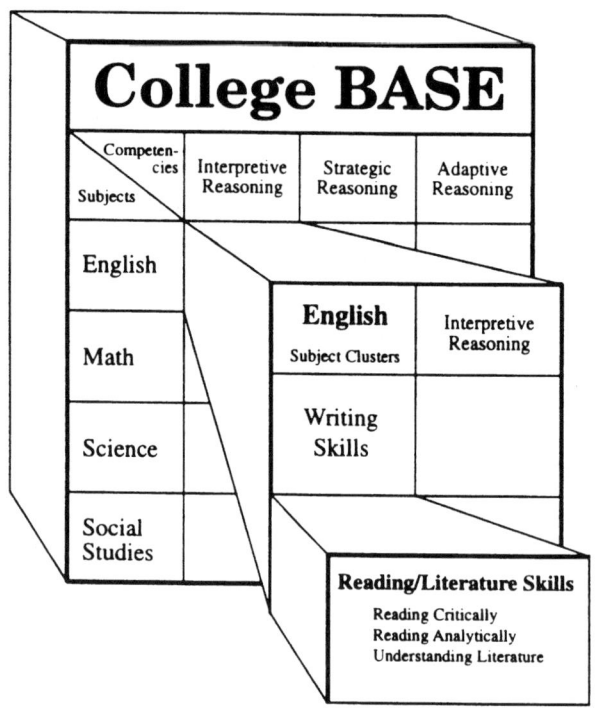

Calibration and Scoring

Item response theory (IRT) is the scaling approach used to determine particular characteristics of items and to estimate examinees' abilities in the areas assessed by College BASE. IRT is a statistical procedure employed by psychometricians to scale (or score) a test instrument. While technically complex, it offers a number of advantages over traditional scaling techniques (Hambleton 1996). Its primary strength is that it allows more precise measuring of an examinee's ability in a given construct. Compared to traditional scaling methods, IRT yields more *information* with less *error*.

Technically, item responses in College BASE are calibrated and scored using a two-parameter logistic IRT model,

FIGURE 4

Item Used to Assess the Skill of Analytical Reading

These boys, now, were living as we'd been then, they were growing up with a rush and their heads bumped abruptly against the low ceiling of their actual possibilities. They were filled with rage. All they really knew were two darkness, the darkness of their lives, which was closing in on them, and the darkness of the movies, which blinded them to that other darkness, and in which they now, vindictively, dreamed, at once more together than they were at any other time.

Why does the **"darkness of the movies"** blind the boys **"to that other darkness"**?

A. The films portrayed lives so much worse than their own that the boys were cheered by the comparison.

B. The blinding despair enacted in the films contributed to the boys' pessimism.

C. The films made the boys so angry that they became blind with rage.

* D. The illusions of the films helped the boys temporarily escape their problems.

*Denotes correct answer.

whose appropriateness for the assessment was investigated (see Osterlind and Merz 1990). Four assumptions underlie the use of item response models in calibration and scoring: (1) unidimensionality of the items, (2) local independence of the items, (3) shape of the item characteristic curves, and (4) degree of speediness of the test (Hambleton, Swaminathan, and Rogers 1991). Each assumption was addressed during the construction of College BASE, providing strong evidence that scaling the instrument using IRT yields reliable and valid interpretations of the scores.

Numerical scores are provided for each subject area and cluster along with a composite (total) score. The scale for these scores has a mean of 300 and a range from 40 to 560 points. The standard deviation for each score is set at 65

FIGURE 5
Item Used to Assess a Basic Geometric Skill

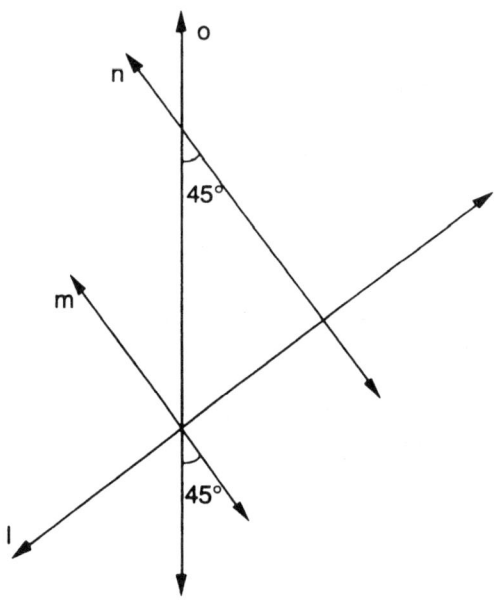

Which lines are perpendicular?

*A. l and n
B. l and o
C. m and n
D. m and o

* Denotes correct answer.

points, allowing for plus or minus four standard deviations within the range of scores. The numbers 300 and 65 were selected as scaling anchors because they would not be confused with other scales associated with collegians, such as the SAT and GRE, whose scales are anchored at 500 and 100 units, respectively. Students' performance on the test closely parallels its specifications. For example, a composite score of 299 represents the 50th percentile on the test, according to published user norms (Pike 1991).

In addition to numerical scores, ratings of "high," "medium," and "low" are provided for each skill area. The distinction among these categories is defined as the point of

FIGURE 6

Item Used to Assess the Skill of Recognizing Principal Elements in an Experiment

In the nineteenth century, Louis Pasteur performed an experiment in which he bent the necks of flasks into "S" shapes, leaving their ends opened. Then he boiled broth in the flasks to force air out and kill any microbes inside. After the flasks cooled, he left some of them upright for observation. Before setting aside others to observe, he tilted them so that the broth moved up into the bent necks and then back into the flasks. After the flasks had been prepared, he watched them for signs of microbial growth.

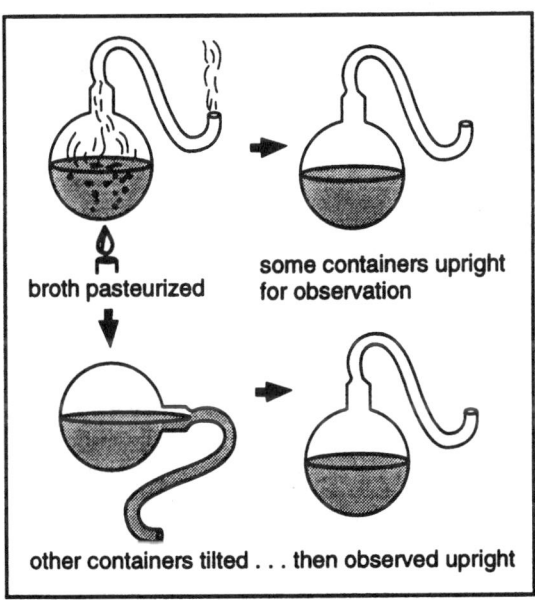

Which hypothesis was Pasteur testing in this experiment?

A. Flasks with bent necks would cause microbes to grow in the broth.

B. Cooling broth in the flasks would cause microbes to grow in the broth.

C. Heating broth in the flasks and then cooling it would cause microbes to grow in the broth.

*D. Contact of the broth with something in the necks of the flasks would cause microbes to grow in the broth.

* Denotes correct answer.

FIGURE 7

**Item Used to Assess the Skill of Recognizing
The Significance of World Events**

Which was a result of the Renaissance?

* A. The boundaries of knowledge and culture were greatly extended.

B. Monasteries and churches were founded.

C. Industry improved the standard of living of most people.

D. New independent nations were formed.

---

* Denotes correct answer.

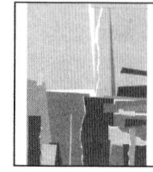

steepest inflection in the test information curves for the skill and competency scores (Osterlind and Merz 1990). That is, it is theoretically possible for all examinees within a given subpopulation to receive the same rating (e.g., "high") on a particular skill. By mathematical coincidence, the cut-score points correspond to approximately plus or minus one standard deviation for the skill and competency scores.

Skill scores are reported in this manner for two reasons. First, each skill on the test includes only eight or nine items, which was judged to be an insufficient number of items to justify a scaled score. Second, this practice is conceptually more consistent with reporting criterion achievements, a major goal of College BASE. Three categories are used rather than a simple distinction between pass/nonpass or mastery/nonmastery to indicate that the skills are attained in degrees rather than in an absolute sense (Osterlind and Merz 1990).

Like the skill scores, the scores for the three reasoning competencies (interpretive, strategic, and adaptive reasoning) also are reported as high, medium, or low, using the same criteria for classification. The rationale for this reporting scheme is that the competencies are a logical construct dictating criterion levels rather than an empirical construct. As conceived, they are multidimensional factors and may violate the unidimensionality assumption to some unknown degree. Consequently, competency scores are reported as high, medium, or low as a gross indication of an examinee's ability to reason, even though a sufficient number of items could be assigned to each reasoning competency to construct reliable subscales for each of them.

New forms of College BASE are developed annually. For each new form of the test, approximately 20 percent of the items on the previous form are replaced. Equivalence of forms is maintained using IRT linking procedures and a set of core items common to all forms of the exam.

Evidence of Reliability and Validity

Studies conducted during the early administrations of College BASE found that test scores evidenced acceptable levels of internal consistency. According to these studies, the KR20 coefficient for the composite score is 0.95, and the KR20 coefficients for the subject areas are 0.77 for English, 0.89 for mathematics, 0.78 for science, and 0.83 for social studies. The KR20 coefficients for College BASE cluster scores range from 0.67 for writing to 0.84 for algebra (Osterlind and Merz 1992). Moreover, the mean College BASE composite, subject, and cluster scores are highly dependable ($X \geq 0.90$) for groups of 100 or more examinees (Pike 1992b). As expected, the reliability indices calculated with the composite score will tend to be high because of the large number of items included in the matrices, while the reliabilities on the subjects and clusters are depressed slightly because they have fewer items.

Consistency in decisions about the classification of examinees' scores as high, medium, or low on the skill and competency scales was assessed using one method (Huynh and Sanders 1980) and estimated again using a beta-binomial model as a cross-check (Subkoviak 1988). Results indicated that the decision-consistency coefficients were sufficiently high to demonstrate that classifications would be consistent over repeated testing of the same group of examinees (Osterlind and Merz 1992). In other words, empirical evidence suggests that labeling examinees as "high," "medium," or "low" on a given skill or competency is consistent and thus appropriate.

The best evidence of the content validity of College BASE is the rigor of the test-development process, especially in congruence of the items to the test's specifications. Specific steps are taken to ensure the validity of the test's content:

1. Developing specifications for test content
2. Preparing specifications for items
3. Field testing items
4. Reviewing the congruence and differential performance (i.e., bias) of the items
5. Selecting items for final test forms based on established criteria
6. Developing procedures for standardizing administration of the test
7. Designing policies for use of the test that enhance accurate interpretations and protect examinees (Osterlind and Merz 1992).

Each of these steps is described in detail in the technical manual for College BASE.

The primary criterion for assessing the construct validity of College BASE was the correspondence between the test's specifications and its empirical factor structure (see also Messick 1989). Test developers conducted two separate confirmatory analyses using different sets of examinees to evaluate the similarity of the test specifications and the empirical structure of College BASE. Analyses were conducted for the subject and cluster scores, and results of both studies indicated that a high degree of correspondence exists between the test specifications for College BASE and its factor structure (Osterlind and Merz 1990; see also Pike 1992a and Thorndike and Andrieu-Parker 1992). Collectively, these studies provide convergent evidence that the test's factor structure is stable.

Studies also have provided evidence of the criterion-related validity of College BASE scores. Consistent with expectations, research has found that College BASE scores are moderately related to scores on the ACT assessment examination and to verbal and quantitative scores on the SAT (Osterlind and Schmitz 1993). These same studies found a moderate relationship between College BASE scores and cumulative GPA. Later, we shall say more about the relationship between essay and multiple-choice scores and grades in college courses.

An examination of the validity of College BASE scores as a reliable predictor of the National Teachers Examination (NTE) scores and cumulative grade point average clearly indicated the superiority of College BASE scores compared with ACT assessment scores as predictors of both NTE scores and cumulative grade point average (Osterlind and Schmitz 1993).

An examination of the validity of College BASE scores as a reliable predictor of the National Teachers Examination scores and cumulative grade point average clearly indicated the superiority of College BASE scores compared with ACT.

Sensitivity of test scores to a collegian's educational experiences is an important requirement for a valid instrument for assessing outcomes (Pike 1989). An examination of the convergent and discriminant validity of College BASE scores compared with students' coursework at the University of Tennessee–Knoxville (UTK) found that College BASE composite and subject scores were sensitive to differences in patterns of coursework (Pike 1992a). These findings were replicated in a subsequent study (Phillippi and Banta 1991) using a different cohort of UTK seniors.

The Students
The data reported in this monograph are based on College BASE scores for 74,535 students tested between 1988 and 1993. Approximately 64 percent of the students in the study population were females, and 36 percent were males. Slightly more than 2 percent of the students indicated that they were Asian or Pacific Islander, 9 percent said they were African American, 86 percent reported they were Caucasian (other than Hispanic), 1 percent said they were Hispanic, and 1 percent classified themselves as Native American. Data on racial and ethnic origin were not available for 1 percent of the students.

Of the total sample, 14 percent were classified as freshmen, 27 percent as sophomores, 33 percent as juniors, 25 percent as seniors, and 1 percent as graduate students. Data on class standing were not available for less than 1 percent of the students. Students in the sample averaged 22.99 years of age. Table 1 displays the number of examinees in the study population and for each subpopulation.

The average ACT assessment composite score of the students was 22.68. The verbal and quantitative SAT score means for the sample were 536.60 and 591.55, respectively. Students taking College BASE had a mean cumulative grade point average of 3.05 on a four-point scale.

The Colleges and Universities
The study population was enrolled as students in one of 56 colleges and universities located in 13 states across the country. For confidentiality, the names of particular institutions are not given, but characteristics about them are. The institutions included large comprehensive research universities and small, private liberal arts colleges. Enrollment at the institutions var-

TABLE 1
Classifications and Numbers of Examinees within Categorical Variables

Classification	Number*	Percent
Total	74,535	
Sex		
Male	28,432	(38.15%)
Female	47,446	(63.66%)
Ethnic-Heritage		
Asian	1,749	(2.35%)
Black	6,681	(8.96%)
Caucasian	64,282	(86.24%)
Hispanic	896	(1.20%)
Native American	727	(0.98%)
Other or not listed	926	(1.24%)
Class standing		
Freshman	10,306	(13.83%)
Sophomore	20,217	(27.12%)
Junior	24,347	(32.67%)
Senior	18,997	(25.49%)
Graduate	703	(0.94%)
Not Listed	517	(0.69%)
Age		
18 to 21	38,058	(51.06%)
22	7,398	(9.93%)
23	4,336	(5.82%)
24	2,502	(3.36%)
25 to 29	6,242	(8.37%)
30 to 34	3,598	(4.83%)
35 and older	5,345	(7.17%)

*Subpopulations within classifications may sum to amounts greater than the total because some examinees did not take all subtests of the complete battery.

ied from fewer than 4,000 to more than 28,000 students. All institutions are accredited by nationally recognized accrediting agencies and associations. About one-quarter of them are doctorate-granting institutions, and three of them are classified Research I institutions (Carnegie Foundation 1987). Most offer graduate degree programs. One institution is a two-year community college. All of the colleges and universities required students to complete a general education course of study.

The colleges and universities in this study are a "user" population; that is, institutions voluntarily selected College BASE for whatever reasons served their purposes. Once they selected the test, they were automatically included in the study population. Within a given institution, the examinees might or might not have been systematically drawn. These haphazard sampling characteristics inhibit the generalizability of the scores to populations who were not included in the test sample.

The Study Variables
In addition to examining the population of students generally, data were also analyzed by subpopulation along four categorical variables: sex, ethnic heritage, class standing, and age. Each variable has distinct features that divide it into meaningful units. (Table 1 also shows the classifications within the variables.) The four categorical variables allow for a full description of the findings from a number of important perspectives.

Even smaller divisions of the population could have been made, such as examining the population's achievement from the point of view of high-ability versus medium- and low-ability students, as indicated by their college entrance GRE or ACT scores. Such finer interpretations were not done for this study, however.

The consummate story of a collegian's scholastic achievement, with everything included, may never be told. Factors such as social and emotional growth are an evident part of academic gains, as are gains in the malleable IQ. It is hoped that other researchers will follow up on this study with their own work to include more and more parts so that the fuller picture is obtained. Typically in research, insight is not gained in one big gulp but in the accumulation of smaller bites. This study is but one small bite of insight into the story of collegians' achievement in general education.

It is appropriate to note an interesting sidelight that came into focus during data collection that bears some impact (although probably minor) on one ethnic group: American Indians. Anecdotal evidence brought to light the fact that students may not have reliably marked the classification

"Native American" within the ethnic heritage category. Apparently, more than a few students identified themselves as Native American because they were born in America (and thus "native born"). This error likely has some interpretation connected to the population's awareness of contemporary social or cultural mores, but it was not pursued. The extent of this anomaly in marking is not known, but because of it, no scores are reported for the ethnic category "Native American."

It is also important to note that references to scores on particular items are derived from a common set of items (that is, questions) that appeared on every form of the test. Because the test has some new items introduced yearly on each subsequent test form, not every item appears on all test forms, and, thus, a single-set-of-items test is administered to the cumulative (and larger) population. Including data only from the common set of items ensures that all score interpretations are only from test items taken by every individual in the sample. Conversely, interpretations of scores do not include some items taken by only a portion of the sample population. Thus, the integrity of the data for the study is enhanced by using this criterion for common items.

A Call for a National Study
At this point in our history of higher education, it would be worthwhile to sample systematically the achievement of students who are pursuing formal postsecondary education. Consider this reference to such an effort a call for such a nationally based research project. Obviously, a multiple-choice test of scholastics, whether College BASE or another instrument, could be selected or developed for such a use. The sampling would not be difficult to design; after all, the units to be used for the sampling could logically be the institutions themselves. About 4,000 institutions currently exist, about half of them four-year, degree-granting colleges and universities, the other half two-year and other postsecondary institutions. Virtually all postsecondary institutions have relatively accurate records about their current populations, which include such demographic characteristics as age, sex, race or ethnic heritage, amount of coursework taken to a given date, and so forth. These data could readily provide the information necessary for accurate sampling. Of course, actually obtaining such data would likely strain most

researchers' political skills, not to mention the logistical and technical difficulties of working from numerous, inconsistent databases.

With high-volume optical scanning devices readily available for use, the scoring, too, of such a national effort could easily be accomplished. Moreover, there also exists an intelligentsia of trained psychometricians available for the accurate interpretation of the tests.

Huge problems remain, however, inhibiting such a national effort to understand more fully the intellectual achievement of our college population. They mostly revolve around such considerations as the high cost, the massive logistics, and the unknown will of administrators and students themselves. Nonetheless, the need for such research is evident, and the call has been made.

THE FINDINGS

Any study involving large amounts of data, including this one, yields a huge quantity of information, and thus the findings and conclusions could be arrayed, displayed, presented, and discussed in many ways. For this study, a particular order of presentation is maintained, which should make the reader's efforts to follow the sequence for presenting findings and conclusions easy. Recall that the four main *subjects* (English, mathematics, science, and social studies) are each divided into *clusters* (from two to three per subject) and *skills* (from five to seven per cluster), and that the analysis of these subjects, clusters, and skills was conducted for both the entire population and for four subpopulations (sex, ethnic heritage, class standing, and age).

The presentation of findings and conclusions is divided into two major parts. The first presents information at a global level for the entire study population and then for the subgroups of the population. Its focus is on comparing and contrasting differences among the major subjects and then the clusters. Except incidentally, skill-level data are not described or discussed in this part. Instead, one can find global generalizations about collegians' achievement, both across subject areas and for subpopulations.

Global findings, however, do not capture the richness of interpretation due the data, and they can sometimes inadvertently offer misleading information about what can only be described through more detailed explanations. Thus, the remainder of this section presents the study's findings and conclusions on the four subjects. Within the discussion of each subject, collegians' achievement is described for the entire study population and then for each subgroup. Findings and conclusions are given for all three data levels—subjects, clusters, and skills—presenting a logical sequence for discussing the massive amount of data.

The two major parts of this section must be considered together, for each provides a context for the other. While the global findings point out the main generalizations that can be drawn from the data, the four remaining subsections discuss findings and conclusions in detail to enhance the reader's understanding of the subtleties inherent in the data.

Global Findings

This part introduces the study's overall findings that represent the broadest level of interpretation for collegians' global achievement in English, mathematics, science, and social studies. It compares and contrasts data for the four subjects and nine clusters. In the presentation of the hard data from the assessment, few findings emerge from the data that are unambiguously clear. Rather, most of the findings have implications showing both good and bad elements of collegians' achievement, echoing other research in the area. A classic study of human behavior notes, ". . . some do [change] and some don't" (Bereleson, cited in Menges 1988, p. 259; see also Pascarella and Terenzini 1991).

The first level of data interpretation is simple mean scores for the four subjects. Numerically, these data are presented in table 2 and displayed graphically in figure 8. Here, the simple scaled scores are 294 for English, 299 for mathematics, and 298 for both science and social studies. An examination of this table and figure reveals that, on a global level, two important features emerge. First, scores in three of the four subject areas are very close to each other, with the scores for global achievement in mathematics, science, and social studies all falling within one scaled score point. Based on pure raw data, then, collegians apparently are relatively strongest in mathematics and only slightly behind in science and social studies. English, however, seems to fall behind by several points.

Before we can discuss these findings, however, we must be aware of a caveat with regard to interpreting them. It concerns "effect size," or, When is a difference between or among groups large enough to be interpreted as significant? Given the very large and homogeneous population, even a one-point difference in test scores can produce statistical significance between mean scores on a t-test or by analysis of variance, suggesting that, overall, collegians are significantly highest in mathematics achievement among the primary subjects, equal in social studies and science, and lowest in English. This conclusion cannot be fully supported, however, and one is cautioned against adopting it too quickly.

Effect size is also concerned with the homogeneity of the population and its size. Because this population is both very homogeneous and very large, the likelihood of making a Type I error (interpreting a finding as a meaningful difference when in fact it is not) or its obverse, a Type II error, is quite small. Thus, in this study, even a slight difference between subpopulations is probably important.

TABLE 2

Ranked Mean Scaled Scores for General Education Subjects

Subject	Mean Scaled Score	SD
Mathematics	299	76
Social Studies	298	70
Science	298	76
English	294	65

FIGURE 8

Relative Differences in Scaled Scores for the Four Subjects

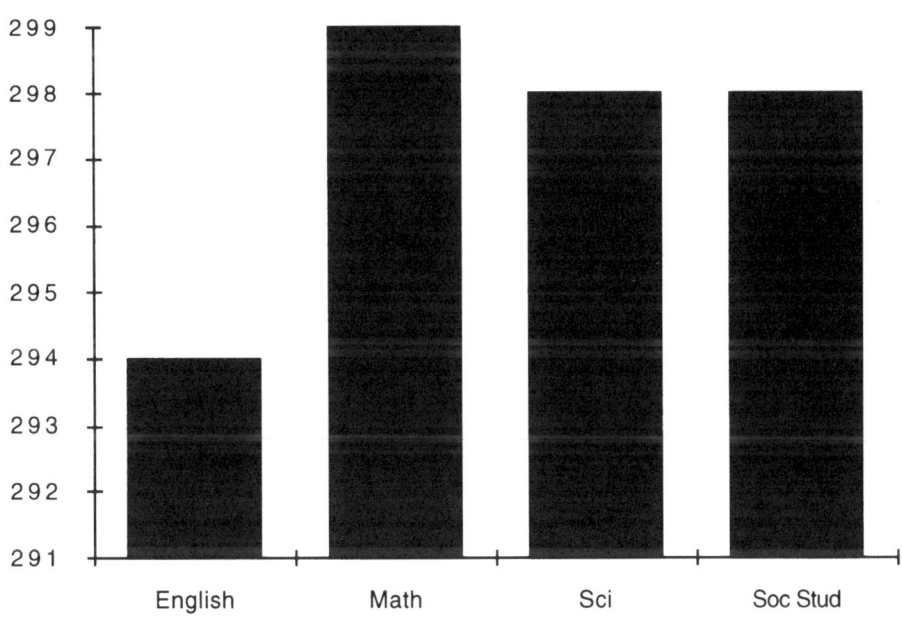

Still, a more precise interpretation should include the fact that just a one-point difference is probably the appropriate criterion because the scores for three subjects are as close to one another as the scaling of this test allows. The reader is thus advised to guard against overinterpreting such small, albeit statistically significant, differences. It is the difference between statistical significance and logical significance.

Instead, a more supportable interpretation of this finding is that collegians have apparently mastered the subjects of mathematics, science, and social studies in approximately equal amounts relative to their respective norming groups. Or in less precise language, college-level students apparently know the subjects of mathematics, science, and social studies about equally well.

For the global English score, however, one is immediately struck by the fact that it is not close to the other subjects. It is four scaled-score points behind science and social studies and trails mathematics by five scaled-score points. This amount of difference between reading and the three other main subjects is hugely significant, both statistically and logically.

The large disparity between achievement in reading and that in the other primary content areas makes up the second important aspect of the interpretation of global scores, that is, the laggardly performance of English relative to the performance of the other subject areas. The interpretation of this finding is that collegians' scholastic achievement in global English is different from, and inferior to, their achievement in mathematics, science, and social studies. It is a truly remarkable finding and is the first time such a conclusion can be made about this population. One gets perhaps the best feel for this "effect" by examining figure 8.

Considering the finding, one may be tempted to ask, "Does this finding mean that students are strong in mathematics, science, and social studies but not strong readers?" This question is a little like asking whether a string is long. Just as the string is neither long nor short but only longer than or shorter than another string, here too, collegians' achievement in one or another subject area is only relative to their achievement in other subjects. This comparison is the relative nature of the findings described earlier. In other words, by these data we see only that collegians apparently know more of mathematics, science, and social studies than they do of English, but what we do not see is whether they know very much of any subject at all. (Understanding that phenomenon is discussed when we get into an exploration of the details for each subject.)

Merely looking at the top layer of the data gives a distorted picture. A dig beneath the surface reveals that the comparatively high ranking in the overall mathematics score can be accounted for by the extraordinarily strong performance of one ethnic classification, Asian/Pacific Islander. This group artificially inflated the mean score for the entire population of collegians. (Further exploration of this finding and consideration of its implications are provided in the mathematics section.) Still, it vividly shows the distortion that can be present in a simple mean score. Throughout this report, we will look beneath the surface for a richer understanding of the data.

Additionally, the global difference among the four broad subjects of general education does not tell the full story of collegians' learning. Levels of proficiency are vastly different among the nine clusters as well as among the 23 associated skills. Further, within any particular cluster or skill, differences are made manifest by wide disparities in achievement levels among the subgroups studied (sex, ethnicity, class standing, and age).

Let us look briefly at the next level of score reporting, the clusters. Table 3 displays, in rank order, the mean scaled scores for the nine general education clusters across all subjects. As noted earlier (cf. figure 2), English comprises two clusters (reading and literature, and writing), mathematics three (general mathematics, algebra, and geometry), science two (laboratory and field work, and fundamental concepts), and social studies two (history and social sciences).

These cluster-level data show marked differences only hinted at in the global subject-level data. The first finding to note from these cluster-level data is the wide range from highest to lowest score, 310 in algebra to 290 in general mathematics, a 20-point difference. Given the very large and homogeneous population, the difference between these cluster scores is vast and dramatic, and represents vast effect differences. The range difference is approximately one-third of a standard deviation for the tested population between the highest- and lowest-achieving cluster. It means that a typical student's performance in algebra is, in relative terms, above more than 22 percent of the typical student's performance in general mathematics. This difference between these areas of mathematics is large and very significant.

TABLE 3

Ranked Mean Scaled Scores for General Education Clusters

Cluster	Mean Scaled Score	SD
Algebra	310	68
Science: Fundamental Concepts	304	64
History	301	63
Social Sciences	299	64
Geometry	298	69
Science: Laboratory & Field Work	297	69
Writing Exercise	297	47
Reading & Literature	296	65
General Mathematics	290	70

Such a finding has the appearance of an anomaly. After all, it would seem, superficially at least, that algebra and general mathematics are closely related in content; one would expect achievement in either cluster to be similar to achievement in the other. Instead, it is not the case: The highest- and lowest-ranked clusters are both skills of mathematics—hinting that the findings in mathematics are convoluted and require in-depth analyses to understand them fully (see "Findings for Mathematics Subject" on p. 59). For now, it is important to realize that, in the cluster-level data, the highest and lowest cluster both belong to the mathematics subjects. Moreover, we should bear in mind how wide the difference in those scores is.

Yet another finding from the cluster-level data, also shown in table 3, is that the two clusters of the lowest subject, English, are themselves both comparatively low. The writing exercise and the cluster reading and literature are, respectively, second and third from the bottom of all clusters. This finding is expected, given the weak global English score. It reinforces what is eminently apparent: Collegians' achievement in the language arts is quite low in comparison to the other subjects. Further, the poor achievement in English is spread across the discipline.

The rankings for clusters of science and of social studies are mixed. Parallel to the results in the mathematics clusters, fairly wide disparities are extant in science and social studies clusters. Again, it raises the specter of attention to careful interpretation of the data, showing that complexities exist for these subjects too.

Thus, it can be seen that the cluster-level findings for collegians' achievement in general education present a mixed picture of their accomplishments, for they are neither uniform nor consistent. These complexities within the cluster-level data will be explored in the reports on subject areas.

Taking the data to one more step of interpretation brings us to the skill level. The overview, using data for the study population on this level, is given in table 4. Using this table, one is able to make comparisons between subject and clusters on the percentage of collegians who ranked high, medium, or low in any given skill.

By ranking the percent of students in each mastery classification, as shown in table 5, one gets an even better view of the large amount of skill-level data, and certain generalizations can be meaningfully deduced. In the rankings, for example, the percent of high achievement for each skill is disparate, from 28 percent for Practical Applications in mathematics to a mere 3 percent for the Writing Exercise in English. Further, the decline in percent of students in the high category cascades downward among the skills, but the percent of students in the medium category is relatively stable. An exception is the Writing Exercise, in which an overwhelming majority of the examinees are classified "medium." A large part of the subject subsections of this report is devoted to these skill-level findings.

Another important aspect of the study derives from the global level of findings: an examination of the classificatory variables (sex, ethnicity, class standing, and age) employed in the study to divide the population into subgroups. Based on these data about classificatory variables, table 6 presents the mean scaled score for these groups, and figure 9 displays the corresponding histograms depicting the relative performance of males versus females. The graphic makes it easy to see that differences in gender pervade collegians'

TABLE 4

Percent of Students in Each Mastery Classification for General Education Skills

Subject/Cluster/Skill	% High	% Medium	% Low
Reading			
Reading & Literature			
Reading Critically	26	53	21
Reading Analytically	25	53	22
Understanding Literature	17	61	22
Writing			
Writing as a Process	24	55	20
Conventions of Written English	19	65	17
Writing Exercise	3	85	12
Mathematics			
General Mathematics Proficiency			
Practical Applications	28	53	19
Properties & Notations	18	66	17
Using Statistics	20	60	20
Algebra			
Evaluating Expressions	25	58	17
Equations & Inequalities	25	58	16
Geometry			
2&3 Dimensional Figures	20	63	18
Geometrical Calculations	16	67	17
Science			
Laboratory & Field Work			
Observation/Experimental Design	18	64	18
Laboratory/Field Techniques	22	57	21
Interpreting Results	25	53	22
Fundamental Concepts			
Life Sciences	26	50	24
Physical Sciences	25	55	20
Social Studies			
History			
Significance of World Events	21	62	17
Significants of U.S. Events	26	57	17
Social Sciences			
Geography	25	57	17
Political/Economic Structures	27	50	22
Social Science Procedures	26	56	18

TABLE 5
Ranking by Percent of Students in Each Mastery Classification for General Education Skills

Skill (Subject abbreviated)	% High	% Medium	% Low
Practical Applications (Math)	28	53	19
Political/Economic Structures (SS)	27	50	22
Reading Critically (Eng)	26	53	21
Life Sciences (Sci)	26	50	24
Significants of U.S. Events (SS)	26	57	17
Social Science Procedures (SS)	26	56	18
Reading Analytically (Eng)	25	53	22
Evaluating Expressions (Math)	25	58	17
Equations & Inequalities (Math)	25	58	16
Interpreting Results (Sci)	25	53	22
Physical Sciences (Sci)	25	55	20
Geography (SS)	25	57	17
Writing as a Process (Eng)	24	55	20
Laboratory/Field Techniques (Sci)	22	57	21
Significance of World Events (SS)	21	62	17
Using Statistics (Math)	20	60	20
2&3 Dimensional Figures (Math)	20	63	18
Conventions of Written English (Eng)	19	65	17
Properties & Notations (Math)	18	66	17
Observation/Experimental Design (Sci)	18	64	10
Understanding Literature (Eng)	17	61	22
Geometrical Calculations (Math)	16	67	17
Writing Exercise (Eng)	3	85	12

achievement in general education. In all four subjects, the differences are highly significant when the achievement of males is contrasted with that of females.

The data for English clearly show that females far outperformed males in that subject. The 18 scaled-score spread is a huge difference, regardless of whether by effect or statistical criterion. From the histogram, one can see the vastly superior English scores of females over males.

TABLE 6

Mean Scaled Scores for Subjects by Classificatory Variable Sex

Subjects	Males	Females
English	283	301
Math	313	292
Science	319	289
Social Studies	323	287

FIGURE 9

Relative Differences in Scaled Scores for Subjects between Males and Females

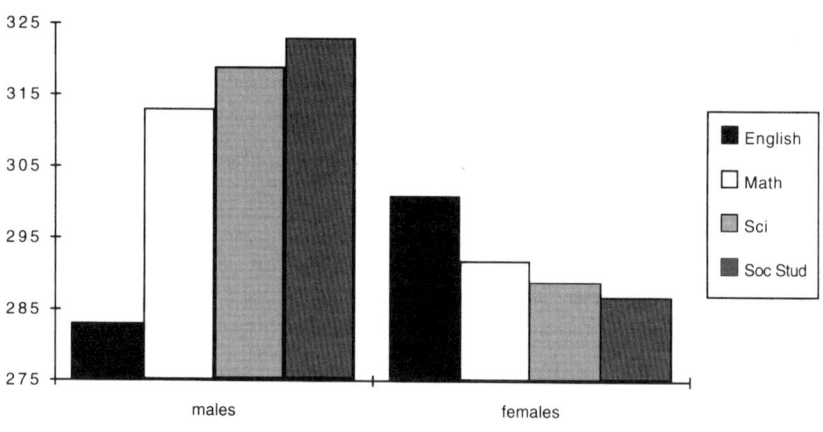

In the three other subjects, however, the histograms reveal that the differences in gender favor males. Males evidently demonstrate superior knowledge of mathematics, science, and social studies over females. Interestingly, the greatest difference between the sexes is in social studies, not in mathematics, where popular opinion might imagine it to be. Here, the divergence of scores is 36 scaled-score points, or about half a standard deviation. For this distribution, such a difference is pronounced. Moreover, among the three subjects in which males outperformed females, the least disparity in scores between the two groups was in mathematics.

The next set of data, presented in table 7, is for the categorical variable ethnic heritage. The data in table 7, as well as their graphical portrayal in figure 10, suggest that wide dissimilitude exists among the races for collegians' achievement in general education. Black/African American collegians appear to have lower achievement for all subjects than other classifications; however, the variances differ greatly from subject to subject. The difference between Blacks'/African Americans' and Asians'/Pacific Islanders' achievement in English is slight, a comparatively small eight scaled-score points. This point is important because it dispels a lot of what many people believe stereotypically about Blacks'/African Americans' use of language.

TABLE 7

Mean Scaled Scores* for Subjects by Classificatory Variable Ethnic Heritage

Subject	Asian	Black	Caucasian	Hispanic
English	253	245	**301**	267
Math	**332**	244	305	271
Sci	281	235	**306**	270
Soc Stud	273	242	**306**	284

*Score in boldface type indicates highest for each subject.

Moreover, as shown in the histogram, differences in interethnic classification are not consistent. For example, an enormous disparity is obvious within the Asian population between their achievement in mathematics and their achievement in the three other subjects, especially when contrasted with English. Within the Hispanic subpopulation, scores for social studies are significantly stronger than those in other areas. Achievement across subjects is more uniform for Caucasians than it is for any other ethnic heritage classification, and it is most dissimilar for Asians/Pacific Islanders.

Data for the classificatory variable class standing—freshman, sophomore, junior, senior, graduate—are given in table 8 and shown graphically in figure 11. Data for this variable tend to confirm what may be the expected outcome—that freshman score lowest in all subject areas, while achievement among the other classes is fairly consistent. One explanation, of course, is that most freshman have not had suffi-

FIGURE 10

Relative Differences in Scaled Scores for Subjects Among Ethnic Heritage Categories

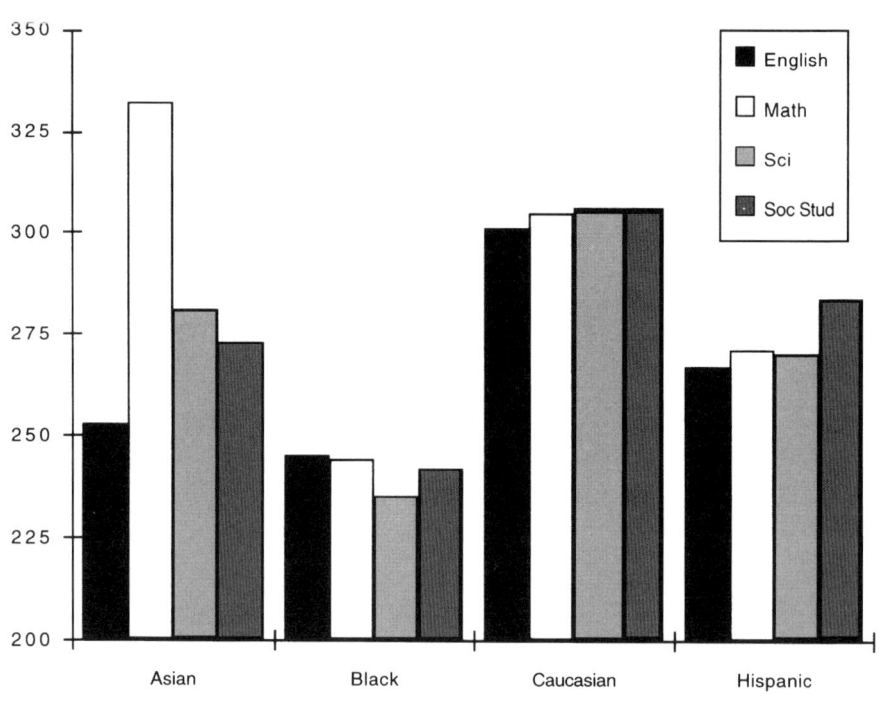

cient college coursework to complete their general education requirements; thus, one would expect this lower achievement. Another finding is that freshmen have the most consistent scores within any class.

Finally, data for the age variable are shown in table 9 and figure 12. As one can easily see, differences in the age categories are enormous, especially for the age group 35 and over. This age group has the lowest scaled score, 271, among all the age groups in mathematics and the highest score, 335, in social studies, a whopping 64 scaled-score point difference. One possible interpretation of this difference is that older students know less of mathematics because they practice mathematical concepts infrequently, if at all, while they typically keep abreast of the news and may thus be more aware of historical events and their signifi-

TABLE 8

Mean Scaled Scores* for Subjects by Classificatory Variable Class Standing

Subject	freshman	sophomores	juniors	seniors	graduate
English	254	297	300	304	**314**
Math	254	309	**311**	296	297
Sci	256	300	**308**	303	307
Soc Stud	256	298	307	307	**319**

*Score in boldface type indicates highest for each subject.

FIGURE 11

Relative Differences in Scaled Scores for Subjects Among Class Standing Categories

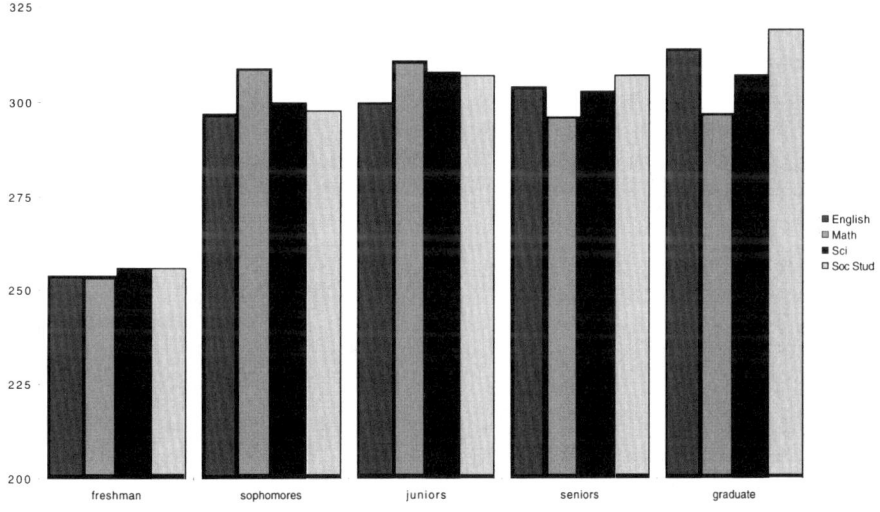

cance. Interestingly, 24-year-olds score comparatively lower than other age groups in all subjects—not what one would expect, because 24 is an age when most students have recently completed or are still involved in their general education coursework.

While a myriad of technical perspectives exist from which one could explore the data, one simple procedure yields some interesting results. This technical approach to the data is to examine the mean percent correct for items, or the mean test p-value, which is the average percent of test items

TABLE 9

Mean Scaled Scores* for Subjects by Classificatory Variable Age

Subject	18-21	22	23	24	25-29	30-34	35 & +
English	294	293	285	285	293	299	**314**
Math	**311**	297	288	286	288	282	271
Sci	**302**	295	291	286	294	293	297
Soc Stud	295	292	291	293	300	309	**335**

*Score in boldface type indicates highest for each subject.

FIGURE 12

Relative Differences in Scaled Scores for Subjects among Age Categories

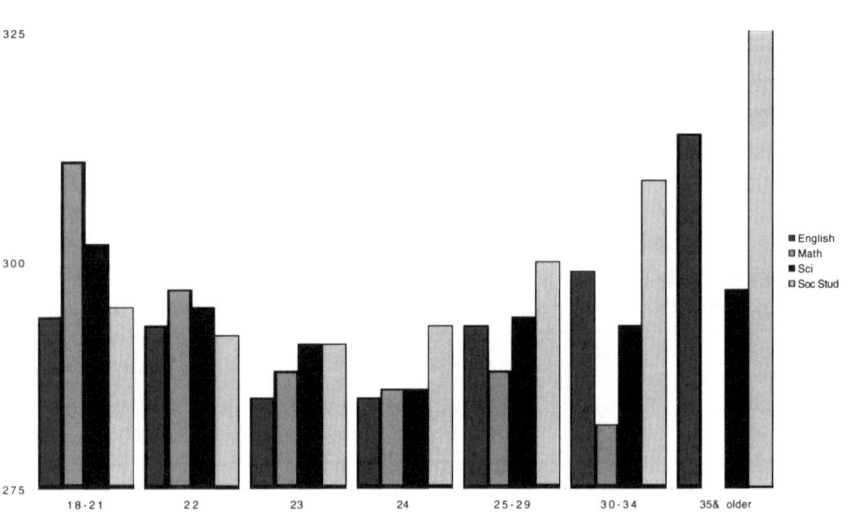

correct for the population and the divisions by classificatory variables. In technical analyses, it is a commonly reported test statistic. Data from this perspective are shown in table 10. An examination of the mean test p-value for College BASE shows the wide range of achievement from this perspective, ranging from .75 mean test p-value for the 18- to 21-year-olds to .58 mean test p-value for the black ethnic heritage category.

TABLE 10

Mean *p*-Value of Test Items for Population and by Classificatory Variable

Classification	*p*-value
Total	0.68
Sex	
Male	.70
Female	.68
Ethnic-Heritage	
Black	.58
Caucasian	.70
Asian	.65
Hispanic	.66
Class Standing	
Freshman	.66
Sophomore	.68
Junior	.69
Senior	.67
Graduate	.71
Age	
18 - 21	.75
22	.70
23	.68
24	.67
25 -29	.65
30-34	.66
35+	.68

For a criterion-referenced test like College BASE with very precise objectives, this spread is larger than might be expected by chance and probably represents true differences. The high group is probably not surprising because it comprises people who probably most recently took their general education coursework. Of course, the high and low groups are not unique but most likely overlap considerably in the individuals included. Thus, it is not meaningful to contrast them as different achievements. Nonetheless, as a reporting variable, it does yield this important finding.

It is important to emphasize that collegians' scholastic attainments in general education are complex and require detailed analyses to understand and interpret them. Thus, it is to a more complete description of the findings that we now turn.

Findings for English Subject

In College BASE, English encompasses three primary disciplines within the language arts: reading, understanding literature, and writing. Experts generally acknowledge that these areas make up the domain, however broadly defined. And while language arts also include many imaginative and creative elements, those vectors are not amenable to standardized assessment and are consequently left to personal assessment or discovery by other means. They are not included in this look at collegians' knowledge of English language arts.

For organizational purposes on the test, English is divided into two clusters, reading and literature, and writing. Each cluster is composed of three skills important to that area. For the reading and literature cluster, the skills are reading critically, reading analytically, and understanding literature. For the writing cluster, the skills are writing as a process, conventions of written English, and demonstrating the integration of writing skills by composing an argumentative essay that is typically three to five paragraphs long.

While the reading score relies solely on answering 41 multiple-choice questions, the writing score is derived through a formula combining responses to 16 multiple-choice items with the holistically graded writing sample. The writing-related multiple-choice items attend to important aspects of grammar and English writing conventions, while the essay focuses on developing ideas logically and coherently with adequate supporting detail. Collectively, the 57 multiple-choice English items and the writing sample make up a relatively thorough assessment of college- and university-level students' proficiency in the area.

As already noted, collegians' achievement in the global field of English is comparatively low—but this simple statement does not unveil the full extent of collegians' knowledge in this subject. To do that, we must examine particular aspects of their learning in English, which we can do by looking at achievement within the two clusters and six skills

...collegians' achievement in the global field of English is comparatively low....

making up the English test. We will examine each of these levels of knowledge for the total group as well as for the subpopulations. Table 11 (with earlier tables) presents the data for this level of analysis. The percent mastery levels (i.e., high, medium, and low) for each English skill are not given in their entirety but are referred to in the text when they are significant.

Let us begin by examining the differences in achievement between the two major clusters of English: reading and literature versus writing. Reading and literature is primarily a skill involving accurate and critical reading, evaluating a literary text, understanding different literary forms and their historical contexts, and identifying major literary figures. Writing is defined to mean rhetoric and composition, that is, knowing and applying the skills of the writing process. Creative expression and novelty are not included in the assessment.

From the assessment of over 70,000 collegians, we conclude there are prominent differences between students' knowledge of the two clusters of English. While one-quarter of the students display high critical and analytical reading skills, a paltry 3 percent of them can write an essay judged by holistic scoring to be "high." That is to say, one in four collegians is a good reader, but only about one in 33 is a skilled writer. This finding is extremely important. From it, we learn of a huge difference in achievement between these two language arts skills. Further, it reveals an astonishingly low number of collegians who are adept at language arts.

The severity of this concern, however, is heightened as one turns attention to the other side of the coin: toward the number of college-level students who could *not* demonstrate even minimal competence in reading *or* writing. These students are the very low achievers. Slightly more than one in five college students are poor readers, as evidenced by their low performance on the two reading skills: 21 percent are weak at reading critically, and 22 percent are poor at reading analytically. Overall, one in eight (12 percent) is an inept writer. Within particular elements of writing, 17 percent are low in their knowledge of English writing conventions, and 20 percent could not improve the clarity, organization, coherence, or style of a text through revision.

Although studies of aspects of collegians' reading and writing are common, this study appears to be the first in which such an appalling lack of foundational language arts

The severity of this concern, however, is heightened as one turns attention to the other side of the coin: toward the number of college-level students who could not demonstrate even minimal competence in reading or writing.

TABLE 11

English Subject and Cluster Mean Scaled Scores* for Total Populati and by Classificatory Variable

Classification	Mean Scaled Score		
	Total Subject	Reading & Literature	Writin
Total Population	294	296	297
Sex			
Male	283	290	283
Female	301	299	305
Ethnic-Heritage			
Black	245	249	259
Caucasian	301	303	305
Asian	253	249	275
Hispanic	267	274	273
Class Standing			
Freshman	254	259	269
Sophomore	297	298	302
Junior	300	302	300
Senior	304	305	300
Graduate	314	319	305
Age			
18 - 21	294	294	299
22	293	294	291
23	285	289	289
24	285	287	293
25 -29	293	298	293
30-34	299	306	296
35+	**314**	**320**	**307**

*Score in boldface type indicates highest for each area.

skills is documented for so large a population. The problem is so comprehensive that it takes a while to fully realize the significance of the data. Even for the dispassionate researcher, it catches one's breath. Analyzing the findings requires patience and distance. It may be somewhat akin to the naturalist who visits what was thought to be a healthy herd of beautiful animals but discovers that many animals are sick and dying. Such is the state of our collegians' writing.

The instant analysis of this finding from a colleague who is also a professor of measurement was, "Well, the students are only reflecting a decline in writing as a form of communication in contemporary society." While true, this analysis does not necessarily provide the complete picture. Obviously, contemporary Americans rely on oral communication more regularly than they do on written forms, but it does not follow directly that the importance of writing as a functional necessity has declined over the years. Comparatively more letters were written during the Civil War than today; for example, during the Gulf War soldiers could readily telephone loved ones. And today, computer keyboards are regularly used for composition by an ever-larger percentage of the populace. Business and government correspondence has increased many times over what it was formerly. Just think of all the faxes sent today, all involving writing. By any measure, writing remains a vital and vibrant skill. The low achievement in the ability to construct good writing by this college-level audience is indeed distressing.

Nor is reading done less often than before. In fact, book sales are up each of the last 10 years, regardless of whether measured as gross volume or as a percentage of the population. And the U.S. Department of Labor reports that 99 percent of adult Americans are "literate." All of these indices point to the contemporary importance of reading and writing.

Nevertheless, low achievement seems to pervade all aspects of the English curriculum as measured by College BASE. Literature is an example of a portion of the English curriculum that is not well known to many collegians. In an examination of students' knowledge of literature, the data classify 17 percent as "high," 61 percent as "medium," and 22 percent as "low." While this finding may not carry the same ring of urgency as do the findings for reading and writing, it is nonetheless disquieting. Knowledge of literature is a central measure of classical education, but as shown in this study, classical education is seemingly lost to career training or other aspects of today's watered-down general education.

Part of our apprehension for this finding of low literary awareness stems from the fact that the questions asked in this category are, by reasonable academic standards, quite easy. One would expect most college-level students to have no difficulty correctly answering the basal literature-related test questions. Many questions in the literature area simply ask students to identify the work of a major literary figure like Chaucer, Rousseau, Milton, or Frost. Other questions require students to order literary movements into their correct historical sequence—classical, medieval, romantic, or contemporary, for example. A few questions ask for elementary comprehension of a passage. None of the literature-related questions require students to demonstrate the much more difficult skill of interpreting a passage or a poem. One is tempted to speculate about the degree of competence demonstrated by students who have shown that by and large they write horribly. Apparently many of them cannot read much better.

Even at this basic level of literature questions, distressingly few students could recognize some principal work of a major author. For example, only about half of them (53 percent) could match Jane Austen as the author of *Pride and Prejudice* or *Emma*. Even with these simple questions, a large number of students (23 percent), thought that Austen wrote the D.H. Lawrence novels *Sons and Lovers* and *Lady Chatterley's Lover*. More than one in 10 students attributed to her the Ken Kesey novel *One Flew over the Cuckoo's Nest*. Questions about other authors' works yielded similar, low results. To make answering the questions simpler, examinees could approach these identification questions from two perspectives: either by knowing at least one work by Jane Austen or by eliminating the other novels listed as not being written by Jane Austen.

In contemplating these findings, it is important to realize that understanding literature is not merely memorizing lists of authors and their works. It is a much deeper understanding of the human condition. Knowing the period and style of Jane Austen would readily lead the informed student to immediately match the title *Pride and Prejudice* with her name, regardless of whether or not one knows the answer by rote. The same important comment can be said for D.H. Lawrence or Ken Kesey or any of the other carefully selected authors used in the test.

Thus, it would seem, academic rigor is not a uniform part of the English experience for most collegians. For example, at one university included in the study, the entire general education requirement for English could be satisfied by analyzing the lyrics of rock songs. Such sophistry is not literature, although it is sometime presented to young minds as such. More accurately, it displays the assignor's ignorance of humanity as expressed in true literature. "Bump, Baby, Bump"—the lyrics of a song collegians were asked to analyze—is not the same as "Call me Ishmael"—a call to the human soul the professor ignored.

This example from a Carnegie I research university is not isolated. Anti-intellectualism, as espoused in the so-called philosophies of devolution, constructivism, and deconstructionism, seems to pervade too many English departments at respectable universities. This study only shows the sad consequences of such instructional approaches. That the mode of instruction matters to intellectual development is documented in many studies (see, e.g., Cronbach and Snow 1977 and Theodory and Day 1985).

The consequence of this misguided instruction is to deny students a rich experience they deserve, and we can see the results of that withholding: distressingly low achievement in literature by a huge number of collegians. The recent high-level *Scandia Report* (Schrag 1997) corroborates that more than one-third of all freshmen entering the elite University of California university system must take remedial courses in English. The low achievement in reading and writing screams for serious attention by college professors, who have the responsibility to offer students challenging and substantive experiences. The fact that so few collegians are strong writers should be a clarion call to revamp much of what is going on in writing. An exhaustive review of the literature concludes that for collegians, "student learning is unambiguously linked to effective teaching, and we know much about what effective teachers do and how they behave in the classroom" (Pascarella and Terenzini 1991, p. 619).

Further, the U.S. Department of Education, which recently hosted a workshop on design of the National Assessment of College Student Learning, did not acknowledge the distressful situation of ineffective college teaching. The committee of the workshop identified three features of setting standards applicable across a variety of subject matters and settings: the setting of thinking, the social dimension of thinking, and the knowledge component. We see all too clearly that the knowledge component is lacking for reading and writing in collegians. Without this important cornerstone to education, how can one expect students to advance in the other areas?

Differences in English achievement by sex

Turning our attention to analyses of comparisons among subgroups of the college population, we see wide differences in levels of English achievement. The profile of college-level students' achievement in English reveals significant differences between the sexes, primarily favoring females. Overall, females outperform males in both reading and writing by nearly a third of a standard deviation, which means that the typical female coed can read and write at a level attained by only about the top 33 percent of her male counterparts (cf. table 6).

The disparity in achievement between sexes, however, is not consistent for the content domains. In some areas, females are far ahead of males, whereas in other areas they are only slightly ahead. Differences in reading proficiency are less pronounced than they are in writing skills. Apparently, not only are more females than males better readers, but many more are also stronger writers. This finding is consistent with an earlier work (White 1985) suggesting that with elementary school–age youngsters, writing may be a sex-linked ability.

Within the category reading, the variance between sexes is most apparent in the fact that there are fewer "low" ability females than males in both the reading skills critical reading and analytical reading. Twenty percent of females are low in critical reading compared with 24 percent of males; only 18 percent of females are low in analytical reading compared with 29 percent of males. Fewer females than males, certainly, are low achievers in this area, which seems to say that females are overall better at English skills than are males on both sides of the coin. That is, there are more female good readers and writers than males, and there are far fewer poor female readers and writers. Conversely, there are fewer females who are poor at reading and writing than males.

A further difference in analytical reading achievement is apparent between the sexes. Many more females than males are highly able analytical readers (28 percent of females versus 21 percent of males). By inference, then, females may be stronger than males at seeing relationships between form and content. This finding may reveal something significant

> *Many more females than males are highly able analytical readers. . . .*

about differences in brain functioning between males and females. It may also relate to another finding about differences between the sexes among the kinds of writing skills known more to females than males.

The most telling difference between males and females, however, is in their knowledge of standard conventions of written English. Standard conventions are elements of writing, such as subject-verb agreement, misplaced modifiers, and choosing the wrong word. Based on the evidence of this assessment, female collegians not only know more than their male counterparts about such writing orthodoxies, but they are also better able to apply them when writing. For example, for several items on the test, students are presented with a sentence and asked whether it should be revised:

> *For some people, a night at the opera, whether comic or tragic, represent just a three-hour nap in an uncomfortable chair.*

The error in the sentence is faulty subject-verb agreement, with the subject requiring a singular verb: *For some people, a night at the opera, whether comic or tragic,* represents *just a three-hour nap in an uncomfortable chair.* Only 46 percent of male students selected the correct form of the sentence from the four choices presented, whereas 60 percent of females selected the correct answer. Given the size of the sample, this spread in percentages is notably significant. In other, similar items, females consistently outperformed their male counterparts in identifying correct revisions for sentences. Clearly, this writing skill is confounded by sex; that is, females perform it differently from, and better than, males.

Differences in English achievement by ethnic heritage

Differences in English achievement by categories of ethnic heritage are even more pronounced than differences in sex. And much of what is revealed in examining these differences is truly significant.

Recall that the analysis of ethnic heritage subpopulations is divided into Caucasian, Hispanic, Black/African American, and Asian/Pacific Islander. And it is important to bear in mind a point that needs constant repetition: that the data presented here are aggregate scores for large groups. Individuals, of course, deviate from the group norm, often by very significant amounts. When one says, for example, that one group is a standard deviation above another group, it is important to remember that while true for the groups, some individuals in the lower group still outperform many other individuals in the higher group ("the law of the individual"). We do a disservice to many people when we merely describe group means and ignore the law of the individual. This sensitivity should be kept in mind in reading the following descriptions of group achievement.

Differences favoring achievement by Caucasians suffuse the English curriculum. Caucasians appear to be better readers and stronger writers than any of the other ethnic heritage subpopulations studied. Caucasians also demonstrate more knowledge of literature than other ethnic heritage subpopulations. For subject and clusters (see table 11) as well as in every skill examined (cf. tables 4 and 5), the score or percentage of students demonstrating high ability is greater for Caucasians than the corresponding score or percentage for any other category of ethnic heritage. The converse also holds true. A smaller percentage of Caucasians appears to be weak in every skill examined than the corresponding percentage of other ethnic heritage subpopulations.

By this aggregate measure, then, Caucasians are consistently more skilled in reading and writing than other ethnic heritage groups. Whether this difference in ethnic heritage can be attributed to cultural differences is a worthy question for study but beyond the scope of this present reporting. Clearly, it would misrepresent the facts to dismiss inferior achievement by various ethnic heritages to "culture" without specifying precisely what is meant by the word and how it interacts with a set of learned skills in reading and writing. It is more plausible to suggest that discrepancies in elementary and secondary schooling may account for some part of group differences in collegians' achievement. It may also reflect reasons based within an individual, such as low motivation or lack of practice in the skills. After all, one can neither learn to play the piano nor become proficient at basketball without motivation, diligence, and hard work. The question of explaining the why of differences in ethnic heritage is left unresolved for this study.

Probing the differences in English achievement among particular ethnic heritage groups reveals that racial minority groups are not merely behind Caucasian achievement as a unified, all-minority subpopulation; actually, their attainments are widely disparate among the minority subpopulations. Hispanic students, for example, outperform both Blacks/African Americans and Asians/Pacific Islanders in reading as well as in literature. But some Asians/Pacific Islanders are extraordinarily proficient in writing skills, and, as group, Asians/Pacific Islanders are more highly skilled writers than are Hispanics or Blacks/African Americans. Simultaneously, nearly a third of Asians/Pacific Islanders (30 percent) are pitifully weak writers, showing a bipolar pattern in writing ability for this group. Blacks/African Americans lag painfully behind other ethnic heritage groups in virtually all areas of English.

The pervading interest for comparisons in ethnic heritage, of course, centers on differences between Caucasians and Blacks/African Americans. In general, for English achievement as measured by College BASE, these two ethnic heritage groups are about one standard deviation apart, favoring the Caucasians. The data show that both groups contain high, medium, and low achievers and that the *range* of achievement within each group appears to be similar. But the data also disclose that the *level* of achievement is not the same across the spectrum of abilities. In other words, if two frequency distributions, one for Caucasians and another for Blacks/African Americans, are drawn on a curve (technically termed an "ogive"), the mean score for Caucasians would lie above the 84th percentile for Blacks/African Americans. The amount of difference represents approximately 34 percent of students, a major dissimilitude.

Achievement for Blacks/African Americans in English skills associated with critical reading and analytical reading is particularly distressing: More than 41 percent of Blacks/African Americans are in the "low" category. Additionally, in the writing domain, a dismal 1 percent of Blacks/African Americans shows high writing ability compared with a lopsided 28 percent of them who are "low."

Hispanics' achievement in English is slightly more than one-half a standard deviation above that of Blacks/African Americans but still lags about one-half a standard deviation below Caucasians' achievement. Returning to the imaginary graph of frequency distributions, if a third ogive is drawn for Hispanic students, it would lie about halfway between the graphed line for Caucasians and the line for Blacks/African

Americans. Along with Black/African American students, Hispanic students seem to have particular difficulty with the writing exercise. Only 2 percent of this subpopulation achieves a high writing score, and more than one in five (21 percent) are "low" in writing achievement.

These important considerations must be remembered in the discussion of achievement by different ethnic categories. One consideration is the linguistic component of students' achievement, which is sometimes associated with particular ethnic groups, especially Hispanics and Asians. The assessment of College BASE contained no data from students about whether English was their native language or a second tongue. Unquestionably, if a large number of persons from the Hispanic subpopulation are not native speakers of English, it could partly explain their low writing scores. Given the overall demographics of the Hispanic subpopulation tested, however, it is unlikely that a sizable portion of them speak English as a second language. Hence, more credible explanations should be sought—another topic for serious research.

The same conjecture about second language does not hold for the Asian/Pacific Islander group, because many of them are obviously aliens, in this country only for their postsecondary education. Probably a high percentage of these students do not speak English fluently, and some are incompetent in English language skills. Given their circumstances, the Asian/Pacific Islander group's scores may not reflect typical college students' level of achievement in English. For them, the phenomenon of a second language could explain why so many wrote inept essays.

The language barrier for Asians/Pacific Islanders can be illustrated by looking at their responses to English language–related test questions. One such item asks students to combine two disparate sentences into a single sentence: *"A store in Seattle, Washington, specializes in accessories for teddy bears"* and *"Bear owners can purchase hats, clothes, and toys for their teddy bears."* A logical combination of these sentences is *"Owners of teddy bears can purchase hats, clothes, and toys for their bears at a specialty store in Seattle, Washington."*

While approximately 80 percent of all other ethnic heritage categories (including Hispanics) could perform this simple combining task, only 66 percent of Asians/Pacific

Islanders could do so correctly. The difference between these two percentages of high achievers is a very significant 14 points, lending support to the notion that many collegians in this ethnic heritage category do not use English as their primary language. Knowing this situation helps explain the poor performance in writing for Asian college-level students.

It is particularly regrettable that we do not have data on this phenomenon of a second language, because it could add a dimension of understanding to our interpretations of differences in ethnic heritage groups.

Differences in English achievement by class standing

The analysis also considered English achievement by class: freshman, sophomore, junior, senior, and graduate student. As might be expected, collegians gain English, writing, and literature skills progressively with class standing, which is exactly what happened for all levels of analysis (subject, cluster, and skill). Apparently, the longer a collegian stays in school, the more proficient that person becomes in the skills of reading and writing. This finding is important and confirms earlier research on the topic (see, e.g., National Institute 1984; Winter, McClelland, and Stewart 1981).

For this study, the most growth appears to occur between the freshman and sophomore classes. Sophomores outperform freshmen by a very significant 43 scaled-score points. The progressively higher scores for increasingly higher class standing continue from sophomore to junior to senior to graduate student. While these differences between class standings are not of the magnitude of that from freshman to sophomore, each is significant.

One might anticipate this finding from another perspective as well. Many colleges and universities require incoming freshmen to take general education in language arts. Because it is typical to take the language arts general education classes early in the academic career, one might anticipate that the skills will improve most right after the courses are taken. It is indeed what has happened. Further, merely being in a postsecondary setting forces many individuals to read a lot more than they might have done before arriving at college.

The findings for writing achievement are somewhat different from those for reading. Writing scores do not gain progressively with class standing in parallel fashion to the steady upward change in reading achievement. For writing, the scores gain only from freshman to sophomore, and thereafter they do not change much. In other words, achievement in writing seems to gain most during the first year of college and thereafter very little, if at all. Sophomores, juniors, seniors, and graduate students appear to write at about the same middling level of competence. A case could be made here for interpreting the positive but short-term effects of the emphasis on writing in general education courses but not in later ones. Seemingly, the farther away one is from writing-intensive experiences in general education, the less the gain in writing achievement, but as this study did not collect information about when a given course was taken, this conclusion is speculative.

Differences in English achievement by age

The final variable studied is age. Overall achievement in English reveals a startling verdict within the age groups. Evidently, English achievement differs significantly between younger college-level students and older ones, favoring the older students. The several categories making up ages 18 to 24 all evidence parallel achievement in English, in contrast to the achievement of students who are 25 years and older. The difference is even more pronounced for collegians over the age of 35, who score highest of all. Each older age category achieves progressively more gains.

This finding is further supported when scores for the two larger groups ("24 and younger" and "older than 24") are analyzed. When viewed as two large groups, older students outperform younger ones in all areas of reading (see table 11). Thus, it appears that, when grouped by age, younger students do not gain very much in reading ability during the years they are in college but older, often returning students do gain quite a lot in reading achievement.

The differences in the age variable for reading do not carry over to analogous age differences for writing. As seen for the other variables, writing scores are mediocre for all age categories. The evidence here also indicates that very few highly able writers exist. Most college-level students, regardless of age, can write somewhat—perhaps even adequately—but their numbers include startlingly few very strong writers, and about 12 percent of them are substandard, poor writers.

Findings for Mathematics Subject

As we saw earlier, collegians' scholastic achievement, viewed globally, is higher in basal mathematics than it is in any other content area of general education, whether science, social studies, or English. Thus, at least superficially, college-level students as a group demonstrate an apparent relative mastery of beginning mathematics. Table 12 presents the base data for the discussion of the findings for this subject. (Like in the discussion for English, the percent mastery for individual mathematics skills is not given but is referred to throughout the text.)

This finding for collegians' overall relative strength in mathematics achievement is, indeed, good news, but more thorough analyses quickly temper the good news. High mathematical achievement by the broad spectrum of college-level students does not appear to be the case. In fact, the high algebra score for the population is distorted by the extraordinarily superior achievement of just the Asian subpopulation, illustrating the careful attention that must be paid to interpreting simple mean scores.

Moreover, not only is mathematics achievement among various subpopulations of collegians widely disparate; their mathematical knowledge is also internally inconsistent—that is, their mathematical expertise does not cover the breadth of the field in any uniform way. Apparently, collegians know particular aspects of mathematics quite well, but their knowledge is decidedly lacking in other areas. This internal inconsistency is true for even the highly able students.

We see this rather up-and-down achievement most directly by examining the cluster scores for mathematics (general mathematics, algebra, and geometry) in relation to the full spectrum of clusters for all subjects on the exam. Ranking the achievement by mean scaled score for all nine clusters on the exam dramatically shows the wide disparity of achievement within specific aspects of mathematics.

The mathematics clusters are general mathematics, algebra, and geometry. The general mathematics cluster incorporates the skills of practical applications, properties and notations, and using statistics. The algebra cluster comprises two skills: evaluating expressions, and solving equations and inequalities. The geometry cluster contains the skills of recognizing two- and three-dimensional figures and performing geometric calculations.

Moreover, not only is mathematics achievement among various subpopulations of collegians widely disparate; their mathematical knowledge is also internally inconsistent....

TABLE 12

Math Subject and Cluster Mean Scaled Scores* for Total Population And by Classificatory Variable

Classification	Mean Scaled Score			
	Total Subject	Gen Math Proficiency	Algebra	Geometry
Total Population	299	290	310	298
Sex				
Male	313	302	318	317
Female	292	284	306	289
Ethnic-Heritage				
Asian	**332**	296	**351**	**328**
Black	244	230	273	247
Caucasian	305	297	314	304
Hispanic	271	263	285	275
Class Standing				
Freshman	254	261	280	267
Sophomore	309	295	321	306
Junior	311	301	319	308
Senior	296	295	302	295
Graduate	297	**306**	289	304
Age				
18-21	311	292	325	311
22	297	289	308	294
23	288	285	298	287
24	286	284	296	283
25-29	288	293	293	282
30-34	282	292	284	278
35+	271	285	268	275

*Score in boldface type indicates highest for each area.

While all the skills are assessed by multiple-choice test items, some of the questions require examinees to perform a calculation of varying degrees of sophistication. For other items, students must use cognitive processing dexterity, which requires some kind of integration, interpretation, or other higher-order reasoning. By common agreement among mathematics experts who examined the test's questions, however, the mathematics questions are at a basic level for the defined skills. None require complex reasoning, and any necessary calculations are straightforward. Formulas (e.g., volume of a cylinder) are provided in all but the most elementary instances. During the test, students are permitted to use nonprinting calculators of all types. They may also use scratch paper. Figure 5 (p. 20) displays a typical mathematics question on the test.

Of the three clusters of mathematics-related skills, algebra ranks the highest among all nine clusters, an indication of relatively strong achievement in this single cluster (see table 3 on p. 36). But geometry ranks only in the middle of the nine. And, curiously, the lowest ranking of all nine clusters is another one from mathematics, general math. This finding confirms the suspicion that strength in overall mathematics is largely the result of an extraordinarily high score in just the one cluster of beginning algebra and does not reflect collegians' true global achievement in mathematics.

It is hard to interpret *why* college-level students have relatively more difficulty with general mathematics than with the more circumscribed subjects of algebra or geometry. It does imply, however, that the more reason-based word problems of general mathematics (involving rates, percentages, simple reasoning in probability, and so on) are tougher for students than are the straightforward computational items of geometry and algebra. An examination of students' performance on particular test items within the clusters lends support to this speculation. For example, the item presented in figure 13 from general mathematics requires students to reason through the probability of a certain combination of rolls of a die.

As a group, only 56 percent of all college-level students responded correctly to this item. While a few students chose distractor A for the correct response (obviously incorrect by even the most elementary reasoning), most of the 44 percent of incorrect respondents were about equally split among the other incorrect choices. This spread of incorrect responses indicates that the students who missed the item are not drawn to a particular distractor by some rational, but faulty, logic. Nor do they miss the item by performing an inaccurate

FIGURE 13

Item Used to Assess a Reason-based Skill in General Mathematics

A cube is painted green on 3 sides, blue on 2 sides, and white on 1 side. What is the probability of rolling the cube and having it turn up blue 2 times in a row?

A. 0

B. $\dfrac{1}{36}$

*C. $\dfrac{1}{9}$

D. $\dfrac{2}{3}$

* Denotes correct answer.

computation. Rather, it appears that they simply do not know how to respond at all. They cannot fathom a reasonable strategy to deduce the correct answer; hence, they simply guess randomly or use idiosyncratic logic, equally distributing their responses among all the incorrect choices. The results on other reason-based questions on general mathematics are similar, thereby strengthening this supposition.

When confronted by a question requiring little reasoning and only straightforward computation, however, the students did better. For example, 86 percent of all collegians could perform the simple computation necessary to arrive at the correct answer to this equation: $4x - 8 = 7x + 1$. These sample questions illustrate the suspicion that collegians can compute simple algebraic calculations but find reasoning problems of general mathematics much more difficult.

Ranking the percentage of collegians who achieved a "high" rating on each of the 23 skills further confirms the wide disparities in achievement within the mathematics discipline. Table 5 (p. 39) shows these ranking data for all the skills. From this perspective, one mathematics skill (practical applications, with 28 percent of collegians demonstrating mastery) has the greatest percentage of students in the "high" category among all 23 skills. But another mathematics skill (geometric calculations, with only 16 percent of students able to demonstrate mastery) has the lowest percentage of students attaining a "high" ranking of all skills regardless of subject, except for the writing sample.

When the 23 general education skills are ranked by the percentage of students who earned a "low" rating, however, a different, and slightly better, picture emerges. The interpretation of ranking skills by the percentage of students who attained a "low" is of course the opposite of that used when the ranking is done by percentage of "highs." Here, the smaller percentage of "lows" in a given skill reflects higher achievement for the group; that is, fewer students did *not* know it. When ranked this way, none of the mathematics skills are among the weakest third of all 23 skills on the exam. Moreover, three of the mathematics skills are among the strongest third of skills.

These findings suggest that, taken as a group, relatively fewer collegians have meager mastery of mathematics than have poor mastery of the skill in other subjects. Thus, we can see that college-level students are apparently mixed in their mastery of basal mathematics. Some skills they know well, but others they have not mastered. Yet when their mathematics achievement is compared with their mastery of skills in English, science, and social studies, comparatively fewer of them are grossly low in basal mathematics.

The conclusion, then, is that most collegians know at least some medium level of basal mathematics (especially beginning algebra), and a few, but not all of them, have mastered particular skills in the broader general mathematics. Still, this conclusion must be viewed in the context of looking at the extraordinarily high performance of Asian students in mathematics.

Differences in mathematics achievement by sex

Like that for reading, achievement in mathematics is related to sex, but this time it favors males. By all means of analysis, it appears that males know more about all kinds of mathematics than do females. Not only do males show more composite mathematics proficiency, but they are also stronger in all the clusters. Further, males maintain this mathematical preeminence across the spectrum of general education skills. In every one of the seven mathematics-related skills assessed, more males than females demonstrate high proficiency. When the comparison is simply males to females, there is little doubt about which group shows higher achievement in mathematics.

Further analysis of this seemingly lopsided difference in gender in mathematics, however, reveals an unexpected finding, one that creates a layer of complexity to the differences between genders in mathematics. The deeper sex-related finding is that the differences between males and females seem also related to ability. Apparently, not all strata of the ability spectrum show the same sex-related differences in mathematics achievement. While there are more highly able males than there are highly able females in global mathematics, the number of low-ability males and low-ability females is approximately the same. If the differences in gender were consistent across the ability spectrum, one would expect not only more males at the high end of the ability scale (as is the case) but also more mathematically inept females than males at the low end of the ability scale. But this is not the case. An equal number of males and females are mathematically illiterate, leaving a higher percentage of females than males to be of medium ability in mathematical proficiency. While most of the mathematically talented students are male, more females than males have a middling level of mathematical prowess. This finding is significant in and of itself.

Differences in mathematics achievement by ethnic heritage

When achievement in mathematics for the population of collegians is examined by their respective ethnic heritage subgroupings, a deeply disturbing picture emerges. Achievement among the various ethnic subgroups is widely disparate. Unquestionably, the most troublesome part of the evidence for comparisons in ethnic heritage is the uniformly low achievement in mathematics by Blacks/African Americans. Whether from an overall perspective, clusters of related skills, or individual skills within the field, Blacks/African Americans do not display a knowledge of mathematics even close to that shown by other ethnic heritage subpopulations on this test.

In overall mathematics, Blacks/African Americans are significantly below every other subpopulation included in the analysis. In the three clusters of mathematics, general math, algebra, and geometry, this subpopulation is again the lowest by wide margins among all the groups. And among the seven mathematical skills assessed, Blacks/African Americans had the smallest percentage of persons showing mastery in every one of them, and they had the largest percentage of persons failing each skill. For example, nearly half (47 percent) of Blacks/African Americans could not do simple statistical computations (e.g., mean and range), compared with about one-sixth (16 percent) of Caucasians who could not do the same computations. A full 38 percent of Blacks/African Americans apparently cannot identify two perpendicular lines from among a set of straight lines (see figure 5).

In no other variable studied is there as great a discrepancy in the level of mathematical achievement between groups than that between Blacks/African Americans and other ethnic heritage subpopulations. In other words, while differences are apparent in mathematical achievement among the variables included in the analysis—one sex scores higher or lower than the other, one class standing scores above or below the others, and one age group shows less or more achievement than the others—none of the differences are as large as the gap in mathematics between Blacks/African Americans and other ethnic heritage subpopulations. This finding is startling for college-level students, and it is should disturb us greatly. In fact, it is a call for action through study and remediation (see also Wolfle 1983, who arrived at the same conclusion using data from the National Longitudinal Study of the High School Class of 1972 [analysis conducted in 1979]).

As with reading and writing, the low achievement of Blacks/African Americans may in part be attributed to inferior elementary and secondary schooling. But low achievement cannot be dismissed as solely the result of inferior schooling. And dismissing inferior achievement with a catchphrase like "As we all know, it's the fault of unequal funding for schools" is a disservice to the individuals who obviously need help. The myriad remedial programs extant in elementary and secondary schools seem to be of dubious value for resulting in high achievement for postsecondary Blacks/African Americans.

The Hispanic subpopulation demonstrates mathematical achievement below both Caucasians and Asians, although it is significantly above that of Blacks/African Americans. Moreover, their achievement is uniform within the field of mathematics. When compared with Caucasians and Asians, Hispanics show weaker mathematical accomplishments in overall mathematical measures as well as in all the clusters and in

> *In no other variable studied is there as great a discrepancy in the level of mathematical achievement between groups than that between Blacks/African Americans and other ethnic heritage subpopulations.*

every skill. As a simple generalization, Hispanics' achievement in mathematics is about halfway between the achievement levels of Caucasians and Blacks/African Americans.

A comparison of achievement in mathematics between Asians and Caucasians is a bit mixed, although it does favor Asians. In overall math, Asians significantly outperform Caucasians and, by extension, every other ethnic heritage subpopulation. Moreover, they are much more able than Caucasians in the clusters of algebra and geometry.

In the cluster of general mathematics, however, Caucasians have a slight edge. This advantage may be explained, however, by studying the test's questions in the context of the language differences between Caucasians and Asians. Most of the test questions in the general mathematics cluster involve some reading, whereas virtually all the algebra and geometry items do not. Algebra and geometry items involve straightforward computation. On every test question in which reading is an important part, Caucasians outperform Asians, but on those in which only computation is involved, Asians significantly outperform Caucasians.

Further, more Asians show mastery of six of the seven specific skills within mathematics. Only in the specific skill of statistical reasoning do a greater percentage of Caucasians than Asians show mastery. And fewer Asians than any other ethnic heritage subpopulation cannot perform a particular skill. As a group, Asians have fewer "lows" in every skill than any other ethnic heritage subpopulation.

Differences in mathematics achievement by class standing

The variable class standing reveals another interesting split in mathematical achievement for the subpopulations of collegians. With this variable, the interest centers on the category freshman. Freshmen are weakest in mathematical achievement among all the class standing groups, which can probably be explained by the fact that, at the time of the exam, many freshmen have not yet had the benefit of general education courses. Given this circumstance, one can hardly expect anything other than the finding shown.

The junior class standing category shows the greatest strength in mathematics, followed closely by sophomores. Again, the likely explanation for this finding is the time away from coursework in mathematics. It is during the freshman and sophomore years that most collegians presumably complete their general education requirement in mathematics. As mathematical computation is a skill that correlates highly with practice, it follows that the farther one is away from practicing it, the greater the decline in scores on a mathematical test. This phenomenon is probably occurring here.

Overall, however, what is shown in the class standing variable is the great change from freshman to senior years. This study did not follow a cohort of students, but it arrived at a conclusion similar to that found by Welfel and Davidson (1986): In mathematics, freshman-to-senior gains are significant by both logical and statistical criteria.

Differences in mathematics achievement by age

The time-away-from-coursework phenomenon is also borne out when the scores are evaluated by the age variable. An inverse correlational relationship apparently exists between a collegian's age and achievement in mathematics. The highest achievement in mathematics for an age-related group of college students is the 18- to 24-year-old group. Although this group includes freshmen, it also incorporates most sophomores, and it is the age group that probably took College BASE closest to the time when they were enrolled in general education coursework. As students get farther away from the time they took their general education mathematics courses, their achievement in most areas of mathematics declines.

The two lowest-achieving age categories are students age 30 to 34, and age 35 and older, respectively. In this case, the interpretation is straightforward. It presumes that for groups of individuals, the older a group is, the more likely the group is to be removed from mathematics courses and the daily use of computational skills, especially those for algebra and geometry.

One final point revealed by analysis of the data is interesting for what it shows about the use of mathematics in everyday situations. For six of the seven mathematics skills, comparatively few students (between 11 and 16 percent) in the two oldest age categories exhibit any strong ability. The notable exception is the skill of practical applications in mathematics. Here, the two oldest age categories have the greatest percentage of students demonstrating high proficiency (31 and 30 percent, respectively). For all age categories, the percentage of students showing mastery of this skill is high. One interpretation of this finding is that general mathematics is a part of the daily lives of every collegian, regardless of age. Because everybody uses general mathematics regardless of age, they show similar achievement. It seems that older students demonstrate increasing mastery as they accumulate still more practice with practical applications of mathematics. This phenomenon appears to be true only in general mathematics, however. In less-used specific mathematics skills, such as algebra or geometry, the knowledge fades with time.

As can be seen, then, achievement in mathematics is mixed across clusters and skills for nearly all the subpopulations, especially for the ethnic categories. This finding helps us to realize the diverse academic backgrounds brought to the subject by students when they pursue postsecondary education. Clearly, this area should be examined by student personnel professionals.

Findings for Science Subject

Measuring collegians' achievement in science is, of course, a dubious proposition. No distinct discipline of "science" exists; rather, what is commonly referred to as "science" is the assimilation of a vast array of bits of knowledge and theories from a variety of disciplines, including life sciences, earth sciences, and scientific methodology. Therefore, to capture this breadth of curriculum, the area of science in College BASE is loosely categorized into two broad clusters: laboratory and field work, and fundamental concepts. The cluster laboratory and field work includes recognizing the role of observation and experimentation in the development of scientific theories, recognizing appropriate procedures for gathering scientific information, and interpreting and expressing results of observation and experimentation.

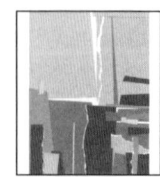

The cluster fundamental concepts of science includes an understanding of the ideas, principles, and theories of both life sciences and physical sciences. College BASE includes 41 multiple-choice test items in this area covering both clusters. Data from the clusters for this subject are displayed in table 13.

Evidence derived from considering the discipline as a unified whole indicates that college-level students display a knowledge of science commensurate with that level of relative knowledge they display for mathematics or social studies. Or, in less scientific language, collegians know science

TABLE 13

Science Subject and Cluster Mean Scaled Scores* for Total Population and by Classificatory Variable

Classification	Mean Scaled Score		
	Total Subject	Lab & Field Work	Fundamental Concepts
Total Population	298	297	304
Sex			
Male	**319**	**315**	**319**
Female	289	290	297
Ethnic-Heritage			
Asian	281	290	283
Black	235	239	254
Caucasian	306	305	309
Hispanic	270	273	287
Class Standing			
Freshman	256	261	273
Sophomore	300	300	304
Junior	308	306	310
Senior	303	301	311
Graduate	307	298	311
Age			
18-21	302	302	305
22	295	294	303
23	291	291	300
24	286	287	298
25-29	294	293	304
30-34	293	290	306
35+	297	290	313

*Score in boldface type indicates highest for each area.

to the same extent that they know mathematics or social studies, which is the global picture for collegians' achievement in science.

Looking within the discipline, however, reveals a much more complex and intriguing picture for students' achievement. Judging by the relative cluster scaled score, collegians seem to have a reasonable grasp of fundamental concepts of science, such as principles and theories of the life sciences and the physical sciences. Their achievement in the life sciences is higher than in any other area of science. By rank, science's cluster fundamental concepts is the second highest cluster of all nine clusters on the exam, weighing in below the mathematics cluster algebra but above all clusters in English and social studies (see table 3).

This broad interpretation would seemingly lead one to conclude good news for collegians' achievement in science. Superficially, at least, it looks as though collegians know science skills fairly well. A closer inspection shows, however, that the happy finding is relatively thin. The data indicate that, in fact, only one-quarter of all students demonstrate mastery of each of the two skills of fundamental concepts: life sciences and physical sciences.

Moreover, the contrary statistic, the percentage of weak achievers, reveals that roughly equal numbers of collegians are, regrettably, very low in these same skills: one in five for physical sciences and one in four for life sciences. Thus, large numbers of collegians, somewhere approaching one-quarter of the college population, are pursuing a bachelor's degree at an accredited college or university with inadequate knowledge of the fundamental concepts of science. Further, because it can be presumed that students whose major is not in the hard sciences take few or no courses in science beyond their general education requirement, one can extrapolate that approximately one-quarter of all college graduates are scientifically unlearned.

Differences in science achievement by sex

Just as enormous sex-related differences are noted for the disciplines of English (favoring females) and mathematics (favoring males), large sex differences are also manifested in science. Here, the difference favors males over females. Globally, males outperform females by a 30-point scaled-score margin, more than one-half of a standard deviation and an enormous difference. It means that, on average, a typical middle-level male collegian shows proficiency in science about equal to that displayed by a highly able female. This conclusion does not account, of course, for the range of scores in the distributions by sex. Numerous individual cases are exceptions to the generalization. Again, the law of the individual takes precedence. Nonetheless, the finding holds true when the sexes are viewed as composites.

Further support for the generalized conclusion of males' higher science achievement is found in examining differences in the two science clusters: laboratory and field work, and fundamental concepts of science. Here, the differences in scaled scores are 22 and 25 points, respectively. These very large differences represent significant dissimilarities.

As follows from the global dissimilitude, the sex-related differences in the five science skills are uniform. In each of the five science-related skills, more males than females exhibit mastery. Curiously, however, the contrary statistics are not consistent. There are not always more low-ability females in the same skills. Actually, of the five skills, only one has decidedly more low-ability females than males (the skill of observation and experimentation), two are a virtual tie (interpretive reasoning and life sciences), and the remaining two have fewer low-ability females than low-ability males—which means that in particular science skills, females may lag behind males in terms of high ability, but viewed in terms of middle ability, more females than males have at least some level of proficiency in science. We see, then, that significantly more males than females are highly able in science, but also that more males than females are inept at science. Most females seem to be about in the middle of achievement in science: Not too many are highly talented, but also not too many are scientifically inept.

Differences in science achievement by ethnic heritage

Examining the data on achievement in science by ethnic heritage subpopulation also reveals wide differences among collegians. Such analyses reveal that Caucasians outperform all other ethnic heritage subpopulations by significant margins; moreover, a large difference separates Caucasians from the next highest category, Asians/Pacific Islanders. In the global science score, this separation is 25 scaled-score points. A nearly equally large gap also separates these two ethnic heritage groups by cluster and by skill.

The differences between Caucasians' knowledge of science and that of Hispanics, the next lower group in science achievement, is yet wider. And the gap between Caucasians and Blacks/African Americans in science achievement is 71 scaled-score points, a difference of more than one standard deviation. This gap in achievement between Caucasians and Blacks/African Americans is larger in science than it is in English or social studies. Only in mathematics is the difference between these two ethnic heritage subpopulations greater. Such a difference reveals huge disparities in knowledge of broad, foundational aspects of science between ethnic heritage groups, especially between Caucasians and Blacks/African Americans. We see that the typical middle-level Caucasian is as knowledgeable in science as the very brightest Black/African American. And like the other content areas, this difference cries out for serious attention by researchers and remediation by school administrators.

Achievement in science between the Asian/Pacific Islander and Hispanic subpopulations slightly favors Asians. In global science, Asians significantly outperform Hispanics but not by large margins. By the measure of the percentage of students in each ethnic heritage category who demonstrate solid mastery, Asians have the advantage in three of the five science-related skills. In the remaining two skills, the advantage goes slightly to Hispanics.

An evaluation of Blacks'/African Americans' achievement in science compared with other ethnic heritage groups' achievement again rings a loud alarm. Not only is Blacks'/African Americans' achievement in science poor when compared with other ethnic categories, but it is also low based on intergroup analyses. For Blacks/African Americans, science is the weakest subject. They are able to show less knowledge of science relative to the standard set than they are able to show for English, mathematics, or social studies relative to the standards set for those domains. A comparison of performance by the ethnic heritage subgroups on just one science item illustrates the deficit for Blacks/African Americans. The item shown in figure 14 was answered correctly by 59 percent of Asians and 47 percent of both Caucasians and Hispanics; in comparison, only 28 percent of Blacks/African Americans knew the correct answer.

Other items reveal similar deficiencies. In fact, for every science item in the test, fewer Blacks/African Americans answered correctly than did members of any other ethnic heritage group. The lack of skills calls for considering appropriate ways to provide assistance where it is needed.

FIGURE 14

Item Used to Assess the Skill of Interpreting and Expressing Results in Science

---

Ocean depth (X) may be determined by measuring the time (t) it takes sound waves moving at a known velocity (V) to travel from a vessel to the ocean floor and back to the ship. Once the time between the departure and arrival of the sound waves has been measured, which formula would give the ocean depth?

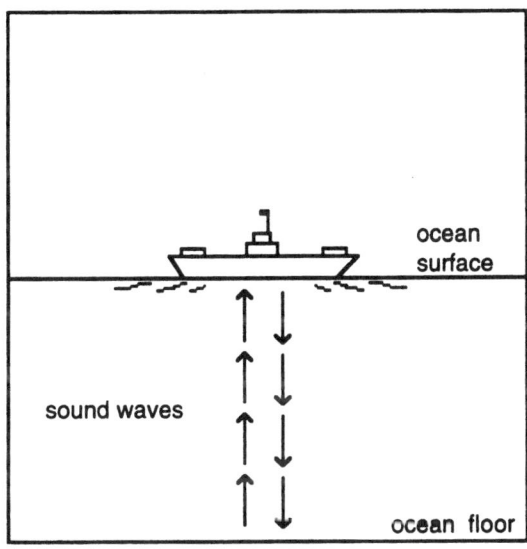

*A. $X = \dfrac{Vt}{2}$

B. $X = 2V$

C. $X = Vt$

D. $X = \dfrac{V}{t}$

* Denotes correct answer.

Differences in science achievement by class standing
Science achievement analyzed by the category class standing produces no particularly unexpected findings. Freshmen apparently know less of science than do the more experienced sophomores, juniors, seniors, and graduate students. Freshmen's low ability is quickly reversed by the time they become sophomores, whose achievement in science is only slightly below that of juniors and seniors. Graduate students seem to make a jump up in science achievement. Thus, the higher the class standing, the greater students' achievement in science. As the test measures general education in this field, one would expect scores organized by class standing to improve as students gain the experiences of more and more coursework, and it is apparently the case in science.

Differences in science achievement by age
No discernible pattern of age relates to achievement in science. Collegians in the youngest age category (18- to 21-year-olds) seem to do better in laboratory and fieldwork than other age groups, but the oldest age classification (35 years and older) apparently knows more of the fundamental concepts of science. To muddy the waters of science achievement further, the highest percentage of students mastering a given science-related skill is also divided between the youngest and oldest age categories.

Interestingly, however, the science skills showing the greatest percentage of students who are inept is also in the oldest age categories. The conclusion of these findings is that for most age categories, achievement in science appears mixed, but for the two oldest age groupings (30 to 34, and 35 and older), science is apparently something known well or not known at all. Few students apparently are in the middle of science achievement for these age categories. Probably this conclusion is tied to which older students have routine contact with science, either though coursework or in some other context.

While this study did not investigate the variable of time away from coursework, one might conjecture that the phenomenon is again operating: The farther one is removed from a content-specific course, the less the achievement, especially for age category subpopulations.

Findings for Social Studies Subject
The final content area of general education evaluated in this study is social studies. Like science, the field of social stud-

ies is an amalgamation of several disciplines; here, it typically includes history, economics, and geography. To reflect this diversity, College BASE has organized social studies around two loose clusters: history and social sciences. History incorporates a recognition of the chronology and significance of major events and movements in American and world history, while social sciences involves recognizing basic features and concepts of world geography and of the world's political and economic structures. It also includes knowing appropriate investigative and interpretative procedures used in social sciences. Data for the clusters are given in table 14. As is true for the other subjects, all skill-level data are not given, but particularly significant differences are described and discussed below.

Because the discipline of social studies is broadly conceived, it is difficult to make particular generalizations that will apply only to the discipline; nonetheless, collegians' achievement in social studies can be anticipated to be on a par with their achievement in the other wide-ranging field, science. The summary numbers on the test bear out this expectation. The global scaled score for the two disciplines is identical, 298 scaled-score points (cf. table 2). This score is fractionally behind the score achieved by collegians in mathematics and slightly ahead of the scaled score in English. Thus, whatever can be said about the global relative achievement of all collegians in science can also be said about their achievement in social studies and vice versa.

Interestingly, however, the similarities in achievement between the two disciplines hold only at the global level. Great differences in achievement between science and social studies are manifested by cluster and skill level. Collegians' achievement within the two social studies–related clusters, history and social sciences, is not wildly divergent as it is for the clusters within science. In social studies, the scaled scores for the two clusters are very close, indicating similar levels of achievement for both areas. Further, the percentage of students who demonstrate mastery of the five particular skills within the discipline is also not grossly different. For four of the five skills, between 25 and 27 percent of students show strong mastery, virtually equal amounts (see table 4). For the remaining skill, the percentage of students demonstrating mastery is a not-too-distant 21 percent. We can see, then, that while science achievement is widely divergent within the

TABLE 14

Social Studies Subject and Cluster Mean Scaled Scores* for Total Population and by Classificatory Variable

Classification	Mean Scaled Score		
	Total Subject	History	Social Sciences
Total Population	298	301	299
Sex			
Male	323	326	316
Female	287	289	290
Ethnic-Heritage			
Asian	273	275	280
Black	242	261	241
Caucasian	306	307	306
Hispanic	284	291	280
Class Standing			
Freshman	256	266	260
Sophomore	298	301	299
Junior	307	309	308
Senior	307	309	305
Graduate	319	322	318
Age			
18-21	295	297	297
22	292	295	293
23	291	295	291
24	293	296	294
25-29	300	303	299
30-34	309	312	307
35+	**335**	**334**	**329**

*Score in boldface type indicates highest for each area.

discipline, the same is not true for social studies. In social studies, the interdiscipline achievement remains fairly uniform.

The consistency is not maintained, however, when the collegians are divided for analysis into subpopulations.

Differences in social studies achievement by sex

As is true for all the subjects, achievement in social studies is related to sex. Males outperform females by a vast amount, 36 scaled-score points. This difference in achievement by sex is larger in social studies by six scaled-score points than it is for any other subject. Further, the discrepancy in achievement between the sexes extends into the clusters as well as into the individual skills for social studies, suggesting that, across the spectrum, males apparently know more of social studies than do females. The differences in achievement in social studies by sex overshadow differences among all other comparisons of subpopulations.

Differences in social studies achievement by ethnic heritage

Among the four subgroups of ethnic heritage, Caucasians consistently outperform the other three groups by significant margins. Caucasians evidently know more significant historical events and understand their consequences better than do the other ethnic heritage categories.

The percentage of Hispanic students who are able to demonstrate mastery of most social studies skills trails Caucasians by only modest margins. For most social studies skills, the percentage of highly able students is in the high 20 percents for Caucasians and in the low 20 percents for Hispanics. Asian students trail Hispanics by rather large amounts. One can conclude, then, that Hispanic collegians seem to know more of social studies than do Asians and Blacks/African Americans.

Blacks/African Americans lag far behind the achievement of all other ethnic heritage groups in social studies. In some cases, the gap between achievement for Blacks/African Americans and the other groups is so wide as to be more than just alarming; it is frightening. As just one example among many, only 6 percent of this racial category could demonstrate mastery of the procedures of social science, compared with 28 percent for Caucasians. A full 43 percent of Blacks/African Americans could not demonstrate any appreciable knowledge in this area. Further, an astounding 44 percent of Blacks/African Americans apparently do not have a working knowledge of political or economic structures. This number of "nonmasters" is more than twice as high as it is for any other ethnic heritage category.

Differences in social studies achievement by class standing

Class standing groups reveal another set of interesting findings. Here, the data indicate a distinct upward trend in knowledge of social studies as class standing increases. Freshmen know less in this area than do sophomores, who are bested by juniors, who are themselves outachieved by seniors. And graduate students top all other class standing categories in their knowledge of social studies. This progression of gains in achievement that goes with increases in class standing is true regardless of whether the point of reference is the global score, the cluster score, or the percentage of students who show strong mastery of individual social studies skills.

Looking at the percentage of students who demonstrate mastery of just one of the social studies skills dramatically illustrates this point. Consider the skill of recognizing the significance of world events. For this skill, students must identify and compare key institutions or participants in major events and movements in world history, or they must identify the sequence of major events or describe their significance, especially as they might relate to broader historical trends. Only 11 percent of freshman but 20 percent of sophomores, 23 percent of juniors, 24 percent of seniors, and fully 30 percent of graduate students mastered this skill.

The relative maturity of each progressive class standing may have something to do with the differences in collegians' achievement in social studies. People tend to read newspapers more regularly as they grow older, and they probably also discuss current events more. And as one get older, one tends to deal with more economic issues, such as loans, insurance policies, and other daily events that may transfer into a knowledge of history, economics, and geography. Hence, achievement in social studies increases as class standing increases.

Differences in social studies achievement by age

The final category for grouping collegians is age. Based on this variable, the subpopulations tend to parallel the finding

Here, the data indicate a distinct upward trend in knowledge of social studies as class standing increases.

for class standing; that is, knowledge increases in social studies with age, and probably experience, as speculated earlier. The highest age subpopulation is collegians aged 35 years and older. Significantly more persons in this group have mastered particular social studies skills than in any other age category. Just like the variable for class standing, however, each group did better than its predecessor in the age category.

These age-related differences are particularly noteworthy in one social studies skill: recognizing basic features and concepts of the world's political and economic structures. Older persons apparently have a broader and much more thorough knowledge of this area than do younger students, as evidenced by their performance on one illustrative test item (see figure 15).

FIGURE 15

Item Used to Assess the Skill of Recognizing the Significance of World Political and Economic Structures in Social Studies

What is the primary purpose of the European Economic Community (Common Market)?

* **A. foster economic cooperation and trade among members**

   B. improve members' agricultural and industrial production

   C. provide a centralized stock market for Europe

   D. regulate currency value throughout the world

* Denotes correct answer.

Barely more than half (55 percent) of the younger age category, born in 1971, could respond correctly, but nearly three-quarters (71 percent) of collegians born before 1958 know the primary purpose of the European Economic Community (Common Market). Apparently, the older a collegian, the more aware he or she is of political and economic systems. It seems that some pseudopsychological component that goes with having lived through different periods of history makes one age group more aware of this skill than another. This sociological interpretation presents a telling commentary on the age-related differences in social studies skills.

CONCLUDING DISCUSSION

Making sense of the findings for this study is a complex task. The data are voluminous, and because the topic is complex, interpretations of the data involve considerations of context and philosophy. Contextual considerations are important because they provide a perspective for interpreting the data accurately. Implications for understanding their true significance are garnered only through a particular philosophical filter—which is not to say that the data are not inherently important in their own right, but rather to acknowledge and appreciate the obvious fact that to judge and value them requires something broader than merely citing numbers and percentages.

No other study has attempted to record on a national scale the achievement in general education of our college-level population.

These findings of collegians' achievement in general education are remarkable when viewed in any number of ways. First, and perhaps foremost, among their remarkable aspects is the mere fact of their existence. To date, no other study has attempted to record on a national scale the achievement in general education of our college-level population. To be sure, Pascarella and Terenzini (1991) exhaustively reviewed the literature but labeled their study "small and limited in scope" (p. 155). Even Wolfle's very large and thorough (and excellent) analysis (1985)—often cited as a seminal work on postsecondary achievement—involved less than half of this population, and that analysis employed a causal modeling method. Another study using the ACT College Outcome Measures Program included only about 1,000 selected students from 10 institutions (Steele 1989). The point remains that large-scale studies are unusual.

Describing this study as a "first" does not deny that collegians are an oft-tested group. Even a casual observer knows that college-level students frequently take tests, and an entire body of literature reports studies on this population using tests of one sort or another (cf. Pascarella and Terenzini 1991). But the tests administered to collegians are typically classroom tests and small-sample instruments, which are markedly different from College BASE.

Other national tests whose names are commonly heard on college campuses are also different from College BASE. The SAT and the ACT, probably the two most widely recognized tests associated with college students, are neither criterion-referenced measures of collegiate learning in general education nor usually administered to college-level students (although they are regularly administered to students still in high school for the express purposes of satisfying a particular institution's admissions requirements and predicting freshmen grade point averages). The GRE, another common test on college campuses, also does not cover the core content of college-level general education; it is administered to students seeking admission to postbaccalaureate training and graduate degrees. And one must include the myriad specialized and professional examination, such as the LSAT and the MCAT. Still, these tests do not assess the general education curriculum, nor are they administered to a broad spectrum of undergraduate collegians. It is evident, then, that the College BASE assessment is qualitatively different from what is done with other tests.

Not only is the assessment of college-level learning of general education courses with College BASE singular; the population included in the study sample is also remarkable. The approximately 75,000 collegians in the study population constitute a very large number of students who contributed data. As a group, they are mixed in sex, ethnicity, class standing, and age, and, as such, they may represent a cross-section of collegians generally. As noted earlier, the students included represent, at best, a haphazard sample. They represent only a sample of students from institutions who happened to elect to administer the test for their own reasons, and the process of selecting students within any given institution is unknown.

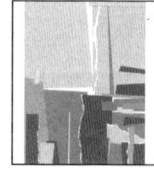

Further, the colleges and universities in this study represent markedly different postsecondary institutions, helping to give the study a sampling of data from a wide array of our nation's colleges and universities. The same point made for individuals also holds for institutions: They are not statistically drawn from the population of all American colleges and universities. The interest in the facts yielded by the study data centers on the enabling capacity to generalize the results of this one study from the study sample to an overall population of collegians. This large number of diverse collegians does provide evidence that these data should be examined seriously as a first step in understanding the achievement of college-level students in general education from a national perspective.

The singularity of this study draws attention to caveats for interpreting the findings. The caveats are also a part of our consideration of context and philosophy mentioned at the beginning of this section. First among the warnings for interpretation is to recognize that College BASE's content paints a very broad stroke for curriculum across all colleges and universities in the nation—a sort of nationwide institutional curriculum, insofar as one exists at all. It reflects a given campus's curriculum only to the extent that its content may overlap the general education curriculum of that particular institution. As discussed earlier, general education is a widely divergent concept on different campuses. In some cases, the overlap between the core curriculum and College BASE may be extensive, in others less strong. Still, during construction of the test instrument, at least 100 colleges and universities reviewed College BASE's content and concluded that it represents important commonalties in their general education curriculum. This agreement on content for the test represents more consensus of a common general education core curriculum than is captured by any other single source—an important facet of the test in itself.

A second, related caveat is the need to appreciate the evolutionary changes in curriculum, regardless of how curriculum is implemented on any given campus. Curriculum is presently undergoing major transformations, quite possibly at a pace unparalleled in the history of American education. While the changes are evident in all disciplines, they do not appear to undermine the fact that, with few exceptions, college-level students are required to take a set of courses that circumscribe a common body of knowledge in English, mathematics, science, and social studies.

A third caveat for interpreting the test's scores is to understand that one cannot infer conclusions about any particular general education course or class within any institution. This link would be so weak as to be spurious.

Yet another caution in interpreting the results from this study is to realize that the scores represent a snapshot of achievement. There are no sampling, methodological, or statistical controls to obviate the effects of differing ability or other relevant variables. Certainly, such statistical controls are important in analyzing results of achievement test–based studies (Werts 1968).

It is important to understand the differences in achievement among the content subjects in understanding the numerical findings of this study. As discussed, collegians' achievement is similar for mathematics, science, and social studies, while it lags for English. We can declare collegians' achievement in the three subjects to be alike for two reasons. First, they are separated by only one scaled-score point, a distance as close to equal as the scaling of the test permits. Additionally, their proximity can be partially explained by an arcane assumption employed by psychometricians during a test's development: that psychological constructs underlying a given discipline are distinct and a particular set of test items can assess only one construct. Technically, learning theorists and psychometricians refer to this assumption as "unidimensionality" (cf. Lord 1980).

A consequence of the assumption of unidimensionality is that the measurement of a given construct is unrelated to the measurement of any other construct. Therefore, when a norming group provides data for the initial scaling of a test, the median score is defined as a center point in the distribution. By definition, the median (or anchor) score for the norming population is the same for all subjects. In the case of College BASE, English, mathematics, science, and social studies all have an anchor median of 300. When a subsequent tested population is very large and is characteristically similar to the norming group, one would anticipate its mean to be near the scaled-score anchor point for each subject—exactly what we see in the proximity of the scores for mathematics, science, and social studies. For these two reasons, then, we can confidently interpret the achievement of collegians in mathematics, science, and social studies to be relatively equal.

By the same reasoning, as well as by using the confidence of statistical inference, we infer collegians' achievement in English to be significantly below the other subjects. Further, achievement in English is not monolithic. Students can evidently read much better than they can write but regrettably can do neither very well: Only one in four is an able reader, and just one in 33 is a skilled writer. The even more distressing corollary to these numbers is that more than 20 percent of collegians are poor readers, or weak writers, or both. And there is no ambiguity on this point: Large numbers of collegians are poor readers and inept writers.

The comparatively low achievement in reading and writing is truly surprising for this college-level population. Remember, the majority of students in the study population completed a general education program of study *before* taking the test. One would expect a large proportion of them to easily display high reading ability, strong writing skills, and a comparatively thorough knowledge of basal literature. But, regrettably, the results of College BASE do not support the hoped-for levels of scholastic attainment.

The finding that so few collegians are adept writers should perturb us greatly. Writing especially cannot be sloughed off as an archaic form of communication. While we live in an electronic age and seem to rely more regularly on our visual and verbal capabilities, abundant evidence still suggests that writing is fundamental to successful communication. Knowing how to read is an obvious ingredient of success in our culture.

Further, collegians' very modest levels of achievement in reading and writing are exacerbated by the finding that they are also weak in understanding literature. This finding reveals a lack of breadth in undergraduate education. Clearly, a liberal education should implant in students an understanding of a range of literature, rich in quality and representative of different literary forms and historical contexts. Evidently, students are not gaining this breadth in their collegiate general education experiences.

Understanding *why*, however, presents researchers a more daunting task. We do not know whether, at the time of this assessment, the disparities between English versus mathematics, science, and social studies existed before students came to college. Perhaps this snapshot of scholastic achievement merely brings to light an antecedent academic condition. Alternatively, students may gain more proficiency in mathematics, science, and social studies than in English while in college. The data from this study do not explore this question. Although national or statewide English assessments with NAEP and other data tend to support the notion of students' low proficiency in English before college, the question has not been investigated as a scientific hypothesis and no definitive conclusion can be drawn (Afflerbach 1990). Certainly, this area is one for researchers to explore.

Exploring other explanations for these troublesome findings leads one to engage in a course of reasoning often based on inconclusive evidence but simultaneously to a speculation that is more informed than mere conjecture. By at least one superficial explanation, the instruction of language arts skills has long been a mainstay of curriculum

Clearly, a liberal education should implant in students an understanding of a range of literature, rich in quality and representative of different literary forms and historical contexts. Evidently, students are not gaining this breadth in their collegiate general education experiences.

planners and experimenters. Yet the results have not been manifested as "learning English" for collegians.

The differences in achievement when comparing males to females is especially noteworthy. It has been widely recorded that gender differences in achievement exist for elementary- and secondary school–aged children. In this study, the differences persist into college-level learning. We also see that such gender differences pervade the curriculum. For this assessment, disparities between males and females in achievement in general education courses exist in each of the four subjects, the nine clusters, and most of the 23 skills. The implications of gender differences in learning for general education are enormous because of the contrary trend in society to be "sex-neutral," that is, treating males and females as much alike as possible. This finding, too, opens an important area for more research, including investigations into learning when such differences begin to appear. And exploring such questions as "Of what are such sex-related differences a function?" "Are they culturally or biologically induced?" and "What can we do to take up the slack for males in English and for females in mathematics, science, and social studies?" will take time for researchers to explore, but a world of literature exists on sex-related differences in college.

One important aspect of this study was to examine differences in achievement for various ethnic heritage groups. Before we begin to summarize these findings, however, we need to be reminded, with a word of caution, about understanding them. Simply citing who is ahead of whom is insufficient to present an intelligent and sympathetic understanding of the data. Stereotypes and unfair prejudices can inadvertently mar interpretations because of the law of the individual; that is, group averages do not apply to any given individual. So before forming judgments about ethnic heritage subpopulations based on these data, one should consider them carefully to eschew spurious interpretations, keeping in mind George Bernard Shaw's comment, "All generalizations are no damned good, including this one!" Nevertheless, understanding the findings by categories of ethnicity or national heritage can provide important and useful information.

As we saw with differences in gender, we see in examining various ethnic heritages that differences in achievement among the groups are large and pervasive. It is especially distressing to report that, by all standards of measure and consistent with every method of analysis, Blacks'/African Americans' basal level of achievement in general education is disturbingly low. It is anemic when considering the global subject level, it is comparatively ailing at the more precise level of content-centered clusters, and it is palpably poor at the definitive level of particular skills. Whether the comparison is by a standardized score on a common scale, by the percentage of students who demonstrate mastery, or by distributions of achievement scores for particular subpopulations, little doubt exists that Black/African American college-level students know less of all areas of general education than do other ethnic heritage groups. Indeed, the evidence is unambiguously clear that between one-quarter and one-half of all Black/African American collegians are inadequately educated in a wide variety of aspects of general education.

This conclusion should disturb us greatly. It has implications for society, and it speaks volumes about unequal preparation for college. The findings are unquestionably closely related to income and opportunity, whether measured by particular households or by communities, as well as to other demographic characteristics. As long as achievement-related demographic characteristics remain so far apart for children in low socioeconomic neighborhoods who inevitably attend poorer elementary and secondary schools, we will continue to see disparities related to ethnic heritage in learning. And this study shows the disparities extending all the way into college.

The socioeconomic situation for too many individuals is intolerable, and it should be changed, immediately and drastically. We simply cannot allow one ethnic heritage population to miss opportunities for gaining achievement in the skills of general education. As this study shows, merely admitting persons from disadvantaged backgrounds into colleges and universities is not sufficient amelioration of a societal wrong.

Class standing is another variable that offers interesting insights into students' performance in general education. As reported, older students tend to outperform younger ones, but caution is called for in interpreting findings based on the variable of class standing. Because College BASE is referenced to distinct criteria under tightly controlled circumstances, it should be installed in a study measuring growth over time. Such a time-related study is certainly worthwhile for what it could reveal about growth in general education knowledge of older students. The present study's design would not allow such interpretations. Further, the students who took the test were not organized as cohorts whose achievement could be tracked and charted from one year to another.

The variables class standing and age lend added support to Pascarella and Terenzini's meta-analysis (1991) of the relevant literature: Extensive evidence suggests that true gains in achievement are made in college.

In conclusion, based on these finding and their interpretations, we see that achievement in general education among collegians is a complex and intriguing arena for exploration. Findings and conclusions are at once disturbing and enlightening. But at least by this national look at the achievement of college-level students in general education, we begin to gain insight into evaluating the quality and effectiveness of American higher education.

REFERENCES

The Educational Resources Information Center (ERIC) Clearinghouse on Higher Education abstracts and indexes the current literature on higher education for inclusion in ERIC's database and announcement in ERIC's monthly bibliographic journal, *Resources in Education* (RIE). Most of these publications are available through the ERIC Document Reproduction Service (EDRS). For publications cited in this bibliography that are available from EDRS, ordering number and price code are included. Readers who wish to order a publication should write to the ERIC Document Reproduction Service, 7420 Fullerton Road, Suite 110, Springfield, Virginia 22153-2852. (Phone orders with VISA or MasterCard are taken at 800/443-ERIC or 703/440-1400.) When ordering, please specify the document (ED) number. Documents are available as noted in microfiche (MF) and paper copy (PC). If you have the price code ready when you call, EDRS can quote an exact price. The last page of the latest issue of *Resources in Education* also has the current cost, listed by code.

Afflerbach, P., ed. 1990. *Issues in Statewide Reading Assessment.* Washington, D.C.: American Institute for Research. ED 360 315. 160 pp. MF–01; PC–07.

American College Testing. 1986. *College Outcome Measures Program.* Iowa City: Author.

———. 1989. *Collegiate Assessment of Academic Proficiency.* Iowa City: Author.

Association of American Colleges. 1985. *Integrity in the College Curriculum: A Report to the Academic Community.* Washington, D.C.: Author. ED 251 059. 62 pp. MF–01; PC–03.

Boyer, E.L. 1987. *College: The Undergraduate Experience in America.* New York: Harper & Row.

Carnegie Foundation for the Advancement of Teaching. 1987. *A Classification of Institutions of Higher Education.* Lawrenceville, N.J.: Princeton Univ. Press.

Centra, J. 1988. "Assessing General Education." In *Performance and Judgment: Essays on Principles and Practice in the Assessment of College Student Learning,* edited by C. Adelman. Washington, D.C.: U.S. Government Printing Office. ED 299 888. 328 pp. MF–01; PC–14.

College Entrance Examination Board. 1983. *Educational EQuality. Academic Preparation for College: What Students Need to Know and Be Able to Do.* Washington, D.C.: Author.

Cronbach, L., and R. Snow. 1977. *Aptitudes and Instructional Methods: A Handbook for Research on Interactions.* New York: Irvington.

Educational Testing Service. 1989. *Academic Profile*. Princeton, N.J.: Author.

El-Khawas, E. 1990. *Campus Trends, 1990*. Higher Education Panel Report No. 90. Washington, D.C.: American Council on Education. ED 322 846. 75 pp. MF–01; PC–03.

Ewell, P.T. 1991. "To Capture the Ineffable: New Forms of Assessment in Higher Education." In *Review of Research in Education* 17, edited by G. Grant. Washington, D.C.: American Educational Research Association.

Giczkowski, W. 1995. "Are Traditional General Education Requirements Right for Adult Students?" *Adult Learning* 6(6): 12–13.

Graham, S.W., and I. Cockriel. 1989. "College Outcomes Assessment Factors: An Empirical Approach." *College Student Journal* 23: 280–88.

Greenough, J.J. 1892. "The Present Requirements for Admission to Harvard College." *Atlantic Monthly* 69(415): 671–77.

Grossman, R.J. 1988. "The Great Debate over Institutional Accountability." *College Board Review* 147: 4–6+.

Hambleton, R.K. 1996. "Advances in Assessment Models, Methods, and Practices." In *Handbook of Educational Psychology*, edited by D.C. Berliner and R.C. Calfee. New York: Simon & Schuster/Macmillan.

Hambleton, R.K., H. Swaminathan, and H.J. Rogers. 1991. *Fundamentals of Item Response Theory*. Newbury Park, Calif.: Sage.

Hannah, L.S, and J.U. Michaelis. 1977. *A Framework for Instructional Objectives: A Guide to Systematic Planning and Evaluation*. Reading, Mass.: Addison-Wesley.

Hartle, T.W. 1985. "The Growing Interest in Measuring the Educational Achievement of College Students." In *Assessment in American Higher Education: Issues and Contests*, edited by C. Adelman. Washington, D.C.: U.S. Government Printing Office. ED 273 197. 90 pp. MF–01; PC–04.

Huynh, H., and J.C. Sanders. 1980. "Solutions for Some Technical Problems in Domain-Referenced Mastery Testing." Columbia: Univ. of South Carolina, Dept. of Educational Research and Psychology.

Johnson, R., J. Prus, C.J. Andersen, and E. El-Khawas. 1991. "Assessing Assessment: An In-depth Status Report on the Higher Education Assessment Movement in 1990." Higher Education Panel Report No. 79. Washington, D.C.: American Council on Education. ED 332 625. 36 pp. MF–01; PC–02.

Kaplan, A. 1995. "Conversing about Character: New Foundations

for General Education." *Educational Theory* 45(3): 359–78.
Katz, S.N. 1995. "Remaking Liberal Education at the Century's End: Problems and Prospects." *College Board Review* 175: 22–27.
Lord, F.M. 1980. *Application of Item Response Theory to Practical Testing Problems.* Hillsdale, N.J.: Erlbaum.
McWilliams, S.A. 1993. "The Sacred Way of Liberal Arts." *Journal of General Education* 42(4): 255–69.
Menges, R. 1988. "Research on Teaching and Learning: The Relevant and Redundant." *Review of Higher Education* 11: 259–68.
Messick, S. 1989. "Validity." In *Educational Measurement,* edited by R.L. Linn. 3d ed. Washington, D.C.: American Council on Education.
National Commission on Excellence in Education. 1983. *A Nation at Risk: The Imperative for Educational Reform.* Washington, D.C.: U.S. Government Printing Office. ED 226 006. 72 pp. MF–01; PC–03.
National Council of Teachers of Mathematics. 1989. *Curriculum and Evaluation Standards for School Mathematics.* Reston, Va.: Author.
National Governors Association. 1986. *A Time for Results: The Governors' 1991 Report on Education.* Washington, D.C.: Author. ED 279 603. 167 pp. MF–01; PC not available EDRS.
National Institute of Education Study Group. 1984. *Involvement in Learning: Realizing the Potential of American Higher Education.* Washington, D.C.: Author. ED 246 833. 127 pp. MF–01; PC–06.
National Sciences Education Board et al. 1990. *A Challenge of Numbers: People in the Mathematical Sciences.* Washington, D.C.: National Academy Press. ED 328 409. 133 pp. MF 01; PC not available EDRS.
Osterlind, S.J., et al. 1988. "College Basic Academic Subjects Examination, Form LC." Chicago: Riverside.
———. 1989. "College Basic Academic Subjects Examination, Form LD." Chicago: Riverside.
———. 1990. "College Basic Academic Subjects Examination, Form LE." Chicago: Riverside.
———. 1991. "College Basic Academic Subjects Examination, Form LF." Chicago: Riverside.
———. 1992. "College Basic Academic Subjects Examination, Form LG." Chicago: Riverside.
———. 1993. "College Basic Academic Subjects Examination, Form LH." Chicago: Riverside.
———. 1994. "College Basic Academic Subjects Examination, Form LI." Chicago: Riverside.

———. 1995. "College Basic Academic Subjects Examination, Form LJ." Chicago: Riverside.

Osterlind, S.J., and W.R. Merz. 1990. *Technical Manual for College Basic Academic Subjects Examination.* Chicago: Riverside.

———. 1992. *Technical Manual for College Basic Academic Subjects Examination.* Rev. ed. Chicago: Riverside.

Osterlind, S.J. and C.D. Schmitz. 1993. "College BASE versus American College Testing as a Predictor Variable for National Teacher's Examination and Grade Point Average." *Journal of College Student Development* 34(3): 187–91.

Pace, C.R. 1979. *Measuring the Outcomes of College.* San Francisco: Jossey-Bass.

———. 1984. "Historical Perspectives on Student Outcomes: Assessment with Implications for the Future." *NASP Journal* 22(2): 10–18.

Pascarella, E.T., and P.T. Terenzini. 1991. *How College Affects Students: Findings and Insights from Twenty Years of Research.* San Francisco: Jossey-Bass.

Phillippi, R.H., and T.W. Banta. 1991. "A Different Coursework Analysis of College BASE Scores." Unpublished research report. Knoxville: Univ. of Tennessee–Knoxville, Center for Assessment, Research, and Development.

Pike, G.R. 1989. "Assessment Measures." *Assessment Update: Progress, Trends, and Practices in Higher Education* 1(1): 10–12.

———. 1991. "Assessment Measures: College BASE." *Assessment Update: Progress, Trends, and Practices in Higher Education* 3(1): 6–7.

———. 1992a. "The Components of Construct Validity: A Comparison of Two Measures of General Education Outcomes." *Journal of General Education* 41: 130–60.

———. 1992b. "A Generalizability Analysis of the College Basic Academic Subjects Examination." Unpublished research report. Knoxville: Univ. of Tennessee–Knoxville, Center for Assessment, Research, and Development.

Project on Strong Foundations for General Education. 1994. *Strong Foundations: Twelve Principles for Effective General Education Programs.* Washington, D.C.: Association of American Colleges. ED 367 250. 90 pp. MF–01; PC not available EDRS.

Resource Group on Adult Literacy and Lifelong Learning. 1991. "Interim Report on Adult Literacy and Lifelong Learning. Measuring Progress toward the National Education Goals: Potential Indicators and Measurement Strategies." Washington, D.C.: U.S. Government Printing Office. ED 334 278. 40 pp. MF–01; PC–02.

Schrag, P. October 1997. "The Near-Myth of Our Failing Schools." *Atlantic Monthly* 280(4): 72–80.

Sims, S.J. 1992. *Student Outcomes Assessment: A Historical Review and Guide to Program Development.* New York: Greenwood Press.

Southern Regional Education Board. 1985. "Access to Quality Undergraduate Education." Atlanta: Author. ED 260 662. 19 pp. MF–01; PC–01.

Steele, J. 1989. "Evaluating College Programs Using Measures of Student Achievement and Growth." *Educational Evaluation and Policy Analysis* 11(3): 357–75.

Study Group on the Conditions of Excellence in American Higher Education. 1984. *Involvement in Learning.* Washington, D.C.: U.S. Government Printing Office. ED 246 833. 127 pp. MF–01; PC–06.

Subkoviak, M. 1988. "A Practitioner's Guide to Computation and Interpretation of Reliability Indices for Mastery Tests." *Journal of Educational Measurement* 25: 47–55.

Theodory, G., and R. Day. 1985. "The Association of Professors' Style, Trait, and Anxiety, and Experiences with Students' Grades." *American Educational Research Journal* 22: 123–33.

Thorndike, R.M., and J.M. Andrieu-Parker. 1992. "Growth in Knowledge: A Two-Year Longitudinal Study of Changes in Scores on the College Basic Academic Subjects Examination." Paper presented at the 1992 Annual Meeting of the American Educational Research Association, April, San Francisco, California.

U.S. Department of Education, National Center for Education Statistics. 1992. *The National Assessment of College Student Learning: Identification of the Skills to Be Taught, Learned, and Assessed.* Research and Development Report NCES 94-286. Washington, D.C.: U.S. Government Printing Office. ED 372 717. 321 pp. MF–01; PC–13.

"*U.S. News* Addresses Flaws in College Guide—Sort Of." 7 September 1995. *Wall Street Journal.*

Welfel, E., and M. Davidson. 1986. *Four Years Later: A Longitudinal Study of the Development of Reflective Judgment during the College Years.* Chicago: Spencer Foundation.

Werts, C.E. 1968. "The Partitioning of Variance in School Effects Studies." *American Educational Research Journal* 5(3): 311–18.

White, E.M. 1985. *Teaching and Assessing Writing.* San Francisco: Jossey-Bass.

Wingspread Group on Higher Education. 1993. *An American Imperative: Higher Expectations for Higher Education. An Open*

Letter to Those Concerned about the American Future. Johnson Foundation. ISBN 0-9639160-0-9.

Winter, D., D. McClelland, and A. Stewart. 1981. *A New Case for the Liberal Arts: Assessing Institutional Goals and Student Development.* San Francisco: Jossey-Bass.

Wolfle, L. 1983. "Postsecondary Educational Attainment among Whites and Blacks." American Educational Research Journal 22: 501–25.

———. 1985. "Applications of Causal Models in Higher Education." In *Higher Education: Handbook of Theory and Research.* Vol. 1, edited by J. Smart. New York: Agathon.

INDEX

A

Academic Profile, 11
ACT College Outcome Measures Program, 81
adaptive reasoning, 17
age
    differences in achievement by, 58, 67–68, 74, 78–80
algebra
    cluster, 59
    ranks highest among all mathematics-related skills, 61
American Indian
    percentage of total sample, 25
    students may not have reliably identified self as, 27–28
A Nation at Risk, 1
anchor score, 84
anti-intellectualism pervades English departments, 51
Asian subpopulation
    mathematics achievement, 41
    mathematics standing, 66
    mathematics students' high performance, 63
    percentage of total sample, 25
    problems in use of English as second language, 56–57
    reading ability connection with mathematics scores, 66
    science achievement, 72
    writing skills extraordinary proficiency, 55
Association for Supervision and Curriculum Development, 15
Association of American Colleges (1985)
    report critical of quality of higher education, 2

B

"Best College Rankings"
    omits information on undesirable characteristics, 3
beta-binomial model, 23
Blacks/African Americans subpopulation
    achievement lower for all subjects, 41
    below every other subpopulation included in analysis, 64–65
    English achievement behind other ethnic heritage groups, 55
    general education achievement disturbingly low, 87
    percentage of total sample, 25
    science showing poor, 72
    social studies achievement gap is frightening, 77–78

C

calculus not included in College BASE exam, 15–16

calibration and scoring, 18–23
campus assessment characteristics and problems, 4–5
Carnegie Foundation for the Advancement of Teaching report, 2
Caucasian subpopulation
    better readers and stronger writers, 54
    mathematics standing, 66
    outperforms all other ethnic heritage subpopulations, 71
    percentage of total sample, 25
    scores more uniform across subjects than others, 41
    social studies performance better than others, 77
Center for Educational Assessment
    University of Missouri–Columbia, 15
class standing
    differences in achievement by, 57–58, 66–67, 74, 78
    supports idea that older students tend to outperform younger ones, 87–88
cluster-level findings for collegians in general education
    neither uniform nor consistent, 37
cluster mean scaled scores and science subject, 69
cluster scores derivation, 16
cognitive-processing
    competencies model based on Hannah and Michaelis (1977), 17
    dexterity requirements, 60–61
college and university sample used in this monograph, 25–27
College BASE
    content as consensus for general education core curriculum, 83
    content validity evidence, 23
    designed to measure recall of factual information, 11
    different because a criterion-referenced test of achievement in collegiate-level general education, 11
    results do not support hoped-for levels of attainment, 85
    specific steps taken to ensure validity of the content, 23–24
    study scope, 5
    subject areas for assessing achievement in, 15
    tests administered to collegians typically markedly different from, 81
    validity as predictor of National Teachers Examination, 24
College Basic Academic Subjects Examination. *See* College BASE
College Outcome Measures Program, 11
Collegiate Assessment of Academic Proficiency, 11
constructivism, 51

Cooperative Study in General Education
    as landmark attempt to assess scholastic achievement, 4
criterion-referenced
    technical meaning of, 29
    test, 11
CRT. *See* criterion-referenced test
curriculum presently undergoing major transformations, 83

D

deconstructionism, 51
devolution, 51

E

Educational EQuality Academic Preparation for College: What Students Need to Know and Be Able to Do, 15
effect size, 32
enabling subskills, 17
English
    differences in achievement by age, 58
    differences in achievement by class standing, 57–58
    differences in achievement by ethnic heritage, 53–57
    differences in achievement by sex, 52–53
    disciplines, 46
    findings as subject, 46–52
    proficiency low before college, 85
    score difference from other subjects hugely significant, 34
    Subject and Cluster Mean Scaled Scores, 48
ethnic heritage
    differences in achievement by, 53–57, 64–66, 71–72, 77–78
exam hierarchical design, 18

F

factual
    knowledge difference from facts, 12
    recall importance, 12
females. *See also* sex
    achievement contrasted with that of males, 37, 39
    better able to apply standard conventions of written English, 53
    mathematical prowess at middling level, 64
    outperform males in both reading and writing, 52
    percentage of total sample, 25
    science achievement seems to be about in the middle, 71

focal point of many criticisms
  general education or liberal studies programs, 3
fundamental concepts cluster, 68

G

gender differences in achievement, implications of, 86
general education or liberal studies programs, 6–9
  focal point of many criticisms, 3
general education skills
  percent of students in each mastery classification for, 38
  percent ranking in each mastery classification for, 39
generalizations, George Bernard Shaw on, 86
general mathematics cluster, 59
geometric skill, item used to assess basic, 20
geometry cluster, 59
global findings sometimes offer misleading information, 31
GRE
  does not cover the core content of college-level general education, 82
  problems of achievement-related research using, 5

H

Hannah and Michaelis (1977)
  cognitive-processing competencies model based on, 17
Harvard University
  admission requirements in 1892 before general education, 7–8
  current admission requirements at, 8
Hispanic subpopulation
  many have difficulty with the writing exercise, 56
  mathematics standing, 65–66
  outperform both Blacks and Asians/Pacific Islanders in reading as well as in literature, 55
  percentage of total sample, 25
  science achievement by, 72
  social science scores significantly stronger, 41
  social studies skills closely trail Caucasians, 77
history cluster, 75

I

intelligence, psychologists' use of the word, 7
IRT. *See* item response theory
item response

models underlying assumptions, 19
theory yields more information with less error, 18

K
knowledge of standard conventions of written English
    females know more about and are better able to apply, 53

L
laboratory and field work cluster, 68
law of the individual
    that group averages do not apply to any given individual, 86
life sciences achievement higher than in other areas of science, 70
Lilly Foundation Project on Strong Foundations for General Education
    12 principles for program of, 7
literature
    deficiencies in knowledge of, 49–51
LSAT does not assess general education curriculum nor is it
    administered to a broad spectrum of undergraduates, 82

M
Malcolm Baldrige National Quality Awards
    plans to recognize excellence in education through, xi
males, percentage of total sample, 25. *See also* females *and* sex
mathematically talented students mostly are male, 64
mathematics
    clusters, 59
    differences in achievement by age, 67–68
    differences in achievement by class standing, 66–67
    differences in achievement by ethnic heritage, 64–66
    differences in achievement by sex, 63–64
    strength from extraordinarily high score in just one
        cluster and does not reflect true global achievement, 61
    subject and cluster mean scaled scores for total population
        and by classificatory variables, 60
MCAT does not assess general education curriculum nor is it
    administered to a broad spectrum of undergraduates, 82
mean scale scores for subjects by classificatory variable by
    age, 44
    class standing, 43
    ethnic heritage, 41
    sex, 40
mean scores
    do not reflect any given individual, 13–14

possibility of misinterpretation of, 13
measurement of a given construct unrelated to the measurement of
    any other construct, 84

N

National Assessment of College Student Learning
    workshop on design of, 51
National Governors Association (1986)
    issue of report critical of quality of higher education, 2
national study
    call for, 28–29
National Teachers Examination, 24
norming population, 13
norm-referenced test cannot yield criterion-reference information, 11
NRT. *See* norm-referenced test
NTE. *See* National Teachers Examination

O

older students
    lowest score in mathematics and highest in social studies, 42
    should use College BASE to measure growth over time,
        87–88
outcomes assessment
    survey indicates 82 percent of America's colleges and
        universities implementing, 2

P

Pascarella and Terenzini (1991)
    review of literature, 81
    meta-analysis (1991) of relevant literature
        variables class standing and age lend support to, 88
Pennsylvania Study
    landmark attempt to assess students' scholastic achievement
        during their college
        career, 4
performance-based funding for public higher education institutions
    state plans for, xi
point of steepest inflection in the test information curves, 20, 21
popular college admissions tests
    problems of achievement-related research using, 5

R

reading

ability connected with local scores in mathematics for
Asian subpopulation, 66
achievement rises by class standing, 57–58
reasoning competencies, 17
rationale for manner of reporting scores, 22–23
relative differences in scaled scores for subjects among
age categories, 44
class standing categories, 43
ethnic heritage categories, 42
sex categories, 40
reliability and validity evidence, 23–25
Resource Group on Adult Literacy and Lifelong Learning
lack of information on ability of college graduates, 3

S
SAT
neither criterion-referenced measure of collegiate learning
nor administered to college-level students, 81
Scandia Report
more than one-third of freshmen entering the University of
California system take remedial English courses, 51
science
achievement complex within the discipline, 70
differences from social studies on cluster and skill level, 75
differences in achievement by age, 74
differences in achievement by class standing, 74
differences in achievement by ethnic heritage, 71–72
differences in achievement by sex, 70–71
findings, 68–70
scientifically unlearned
approximately one-quarter of all college graduates are, 70
scores
as snapshot of achievement lacking statistical controls, 83
setting standards, three features of, 51
sex differences in achievement, 52–53, 63–64, 70–71, 77
sex-neutral trend in society, 86
Shaw, George Bernard
on generalizations, 86
simple mean score
example of the distortion that can be present in, 35
skill scores rationale for manner of reporting, 22
social science cluster, 75
social studies

amalgam of several disciplines, 74–75
differences in achievement by age, 78–80
differences in achievement by class standing, 78
differences in achievement by ethnic heritage, 77–78
differences in achievement by sex, 77
findings, 74–75, 77
knowledge increases as class standing increases, 78
males outperform females by a vast amount in, 77
Southern Regional Education Board (1985), 2
Stanford University, general education at, 6
statistical significance and logical significance difference, 34
strategic reasoning, 17
student sample used in College BASE, 25
Study Group on the Conditions of Excellence in American Higher Education (1984), 2
subject areas for assessing achievement in College BASE, 15
subpopulation variables of sample used in College BASE, 27–28
"success meter" for parents
sending a son or daughter to college as, 1
synthesis and evaluation, 17

T
Thomas Aquinas University, general education at, 6–7

U
unidimensionality assumption, 84
University of California system remedial English courses
more than one-third of entering freshmen must take, 51
University of Missouri–Columbia
Center for Educational Assessment, 15
University of Tennessee–Knoxville College BASE scores at
examination of convergent and discriminant validity of, 25
U.S. Department of Education
did not acknowledge ineffective college teaching, 51
U.S. News & World Reports "Best College Rankings," 3

V
value of a college experience, growing disaffection with the, 1

W
Wingspread Group (1993) report on higher education, 2
Wolfle (1985)
large and thorough analysis of postsecondary achievement, 81

writing
> achievement gain only from freshman to sophomore, 58
> findings perturbing of low scores in, 85
> first study documenting lack in such a large population, 47–49

Y
Yalta Conference example of temporal placement
> as factual knowledge, 12

ASHE-ERIC HIGHER EDUCATION REPORTS

Since 1983, the Association for the Study of Higher Education (ASHE) and the Educational Resources Information Center (ERIC) Clearinghouse on Higher Education, a sponsored project of the Graduate School of Education and Human Development at The George Washington University, have cosponsored the ASHE-ERIC Higher Education Report series. This volume is the twenty-fifth overall and the eighth to be published by the Graduate School of Education and Human Development at The George Washington University.

Each monograph is the definitive analysis of a tough higher education problem, based on thorough research of pertinent literature and institutional experiences. Topics are identified by a national survey. Noted practitioners and scholars are then commissioned to write the reports, with experts providing critical reviews of each manuscript before publication.

Eight monographs (10 before 1985) in the ASHE-ERIC Higher Education Report series are published each year and are available on individual and subscription bases. To order, use the order form on the last page of this book.

Qualified persons interested in writing a monograph for the ASHE-ERIC Higher Education Report series are invited to submit a proposal to the National Advisory Board. As the preeminent literature review and issue analysis series in higher education, the Higher Education Reports are guaranteed wide dissemination and national exposure for accepted candidates. Execution of a monograph requires at least a minimal familiarity with the ERIC database, including *Resources in Education* and the current *Index to Journals in Education*. The objective of these reports is to bridge conventional wisdom with practical research. Prospective authors are strongly encouraged to call Dr. Fife at (800) 773-3742.

For further information, write to
 ASHE-ERIC Higher Education Reports
 The George Washington University
 One Dupont Circle, Suite 630
 Washington, DC 20036
Or phone (202) 296-2597; toll free: (800) 773-ERIC.

Write or call for a complete catalog.

Visit our Web site at **www.gwu.edu/~eriche**

ADVISORY BOARD

James Earl Davis
University of Delaware at Newark

Kenneth A. Feldman
State University of New York–Stony Brook

Cassie Freeman
Peabody College, Vanderbilt University

Susan Frost
Emory University

Mildred Garcia
Arizona State University West

Philo Hutcheson
Georgia State University

CONSULTING EDITORS

Sandra Beyer
University of Texas at El Paso

Robert Boice
State University of New York–Stony Brook

Steve Brigham
American Association for Higher Education

Ivy E. Broder
The American University

Nevin C. Brown
The Education Trust, Inc.

Shirley M. Clark
Oregon State System of Higher Education

Robert A. Cornesky
Cornesky and Associates, Inc.

Cheryl Falk
Yakima Valley Community College

Anne H. Frank
American Association of University Professors

Michelle D. Gilliard
Consortium for the Advancement of Private Higher Education–The Council of Independent Colleges

Joseph E. Gilmore
Northwest Missouri State University

Arthur Greenberg
Community School District 25, Flushing, New York

Dean L. Hubbard
Northwest Missouri State University

Edward Johnson
Arizona Commission for Post Seconday Education

Clara M. Lovett
Northern Arizona University

Laurence R. Marcus
Rowan College

Robert Menges
Northwestern University

Diane E. Morrison
Centre for Curriculum, Transfer, and Technology

L. Jackson Newell
University of Utah

Steven G. Olswang
University of Washington

Laura W. Perna
Frederick D. Patterson Research
 Institute of the College Fund/UNCF

R. Eugene Rice
American Association for Higher Education

Brent Ruben
State University of New Jersey–Rutgers

Sherry Sayles-Folks
Eastern Michigan University

Jack H. Schuster
Claremont Graduate School—Center for Educational Studies

Daniel Seymour
Claremont College–California

Marilla D. Svinicki
University of Texas–Austin

David Sweet
OERI, U.S. Department of Education

Gershon Vincow
Syracuse University

Dan W. Wheeler
University of Nebraska–Lincoln

Donald H. Wulff
University of Washington

Manta Yorke
Liverpool John Moores University

REVIEW PANEL

Charles Adams
University of Massachusetts–Amherst

Louis Albert
American Association for Higher Education

Richard Alfred
University of Michigan

Henry Lee Allen
University of Rochester

Philip G. Altbach
Boston College

Marilyn J. Amey
University of Kansas

Kristine L. Anderson
Florida Atlantic University

Karen D. Arnold
Boston College

Robert J. Barak
Iowa State Board of Regents

Alan Bayer
Virginia Polytechnic Institute and State University

John P. Bean
Indiana University–Bloomington

John M. Braxton
Peabody College, Vanderbilt University

Ellen M. Brier
Tennessee State University

Barbara E. Brittingham
The University of Rhode Island

Dennis Brown
University of Kansas

Peter McE. Buchanan
Council for Advancement and Support of Education

Patricia Carter
University of Michigan

John A. Centra
Syracuse University

Arthur W. Chickering
George Mason University

Darrel A. Clowes
Virginia Polytechnic Institute and State University

Cynthia S. Dickens
Mississippi State University

Deborah M. DiCroce
Piedmont Virginia Community College

Sarah M. Dinham
University of Arizona

Kenneth A. Feldman
State University of New York–Stony Brook

Dorothy E. Finnegan
The College of William & Mary

Mildred Garcia
Montclair State College

Rodolfo Z. Garcia
Commission on Institutions of Higher Education

Kenneth C. Green
University of Southern California

James Hearn
University of Georgia

Edward R. Hines
Illinois State University

Deborah Hunter
University of Vermont

Philo Hutcheson
Georgia State University

Bruce Anthony Jones
University of Pittsburgh

Elizabeth A. Jones
The Pennsylvania State University

Kathryn Kretschmer
University of Kansas

Marsha V. Krotseng
State College and University Systems of West Virginia

George D. Kuh
Indiana University–Bloomington

Daniel T. Layzell
University of Wisconsin System

Patrick G. Love
Kent State University

Cheryl D. Lovell
State Higher Education Executive Officers

Meredith Jane Ludwig
American Association of State Colleges and Universities

Dewayne Matthews
Western Interstate Commission for Higher Education

Mantha V. Mehallis
Florida Atlantic University

Toby Milton
Essex Community College

James R. Mingle
State Higher Education Executive Officers

John A. Muffo
Virginia Polytechnic Institute and State University

L. Jackson Newell
Deep Springs College

James C. Palmer
Illinois State University

Robert A. Rhoads
The Pennsylvania State University

G. Jeremiah Ryan
Harford Community College

Mary Ann Danowitz Sagaria
The Ohio State University

Daryl G. Smith
The Claremont Graduate School

William G. Tierney
University of Southern California

Susan B. Twombly
University of Kansas

Robert A. Walhaus
University of Illinois–Chicago

Harold Wechsler
University of Rochester

Elizabeth J. Whitt
University of Illinois–Chicago

Michael J. Worth
The George Washington University

RECENT TITLES

Volume 25 ASHE-ERIC Higher Education Reports

1. A Culture for Academic Excellence: Implementing the Quality Principles in Higher Education
   Jann E. Freed, Marie R. Klugman, and Jonathan D. Fife

2. From Discipline to Development: Rethinking Student Conduct in Higher Education
   Michael Dannells

3. Academic Controversy: Enriching College Instruction through Intellectual Conflict
   David W. Johnson, Roger T. Johnson, and Karl A. Smith

4. Higher Education Leadership: Analyzing the Gender Gap
   Luba Chliwniak

5. The Virtual Campus: Technology and Reform in Higher Education
   Gerald C. Van Dusen

6. Early Intervention Programs: Opening the Door to Higher Education
   Robert H. Fenske, Christine A. Geranios, Jonathan E. Keller, and David E. Moore

7. The Vitality of Senior Faculty Members: Snow on the Roof—Fire in the Furnace
   Carole J. Bland and William H. Bergquist

Volume 24 ASHE-ERIC Higher Education Reports

1. Tenure, Promotion, and Reappointment: Legal and Administrative Implications (951)
   Benjamin Baez and John A. Centra

2. Taking Teaching Seriously: Meeting the Challenge of Instructional Improvement (952)
   Michael B. Paulsen and Kenneth A. Feldman

3. Empowering the Faculty: Mentoring Redirected and Renewed (953)
   Gaye Luna and Deborah L. Cullen

4. Enhancing Student Learning: Intellectual, Social, and Emotional Integration (954)
   Anne Goodsell Love and Patrick G. Love

5. Benchmarking in Higher Education: Adapting Best Practices to Improve Quality (955)
   Jeffrey W. Alstete

6. Models for Improving College Teaching: A Faculty Resource (956)
   Jon E. Travis

7. Experiential Learning in Higher Education: Linking Classroom and Community (957)
   Jeffrey A. Cantor

8. Successful Faculty Development and Evaluation: The Complete Teaching Portfolio (958)
John P. Murray

Volume 23 ASHE-ERIC Higher Education Reports

1. The Advisory Committee Advantage: Creating an Effective Strategy for Programmatic Improvement (941)
Lee Teitel

2. Collaborative Peer Review: The Role of Faculty in Improving College Teaching (942)
Larry Keig and Michael D. Waggoner

3. Prices, Productivity, and Investment: Assessing Financial Strategies in Higher Education (943)
Edward P. St. John

4. The Development Officer in Higher Education: Toward an Understanding of the Role (944)
Michael J. Worth and James W. Asp II

5. Measuring Up: The Promises and Pitfalls of Performance Indicators in Higher Education (945)
Gerald Gaither, Brian P. Nedwek, and John E. Neal

6. A New Alliance: Continuous Quality and Classroom Effectiveness (946)
Mimi Wolverton

7. Redesigning Higher Education: Producing Dramatic Gains in Student Learning (947)
Lion F. Gardiner

8. Student Learning outside the Classroom: Transcending Artificial Boundaries (948)
George D. Kuh, Katie Branch Douglas, Jon P. Lund, and Jackie Ramin-Gyurnek

Volume 22 ASHE-ERIC Higher Education Reports

1. The Department Chair: New Roles, Responsibilities, and Challenges (931)
Alan T. Seagren, John W. Creswell, and Daniel W. Wheeler

2. Sexual Harassment in Higher Education: From Conflict to Community (932)
Robert O. Riggs, Patricia H. Murrell, and JoAnne C. Cutting

3. Chicanos in Higher Education: Issues and Dilemmas for the 21st Century (933)
Adalberto Aguirre, Jr., and Ruben O. Martinez

4. Academic Freedom in American Higher Education: Rights, Responsibilities, and Limitations (934)
   Robert K. Poch

5. Making Sense of the Dollars: The Costs and Uses of Faculty Compensation (935)
   Kathryn M. Moore and Marilyn J. Amey

6. Enhancing Promotion, Tenure, and Beyond: Faculty Socialization as a Cultural Process (936)
   William G. Tierney and Robert A. Rhoads

7. New Perspectives for Student Affairs Professionals: Evolving Realities, Responsibilities, and Roles (937)
   Peter H. Garland and Thomas W. Grace

8. Turning Teaching into Learning: The Role of Student Responsibility in the Collegiate Experience (938)
   Todd M. Davis and Patricia Hillman Murrell

Volume 21 ASHE-ERIC Higher Education Reports

1. The Leadership Compass: Values and Ethics in Higher Education (921)
   John R. Wilcox and Susan L. Ebbs

2. Preparing for a Global Community: Achieving an International Perspective in Higher Education (922)
   Sarah M. Pickert

3. Quality: Transforming Postsecondary Education (923)
   Ellen Earle Chaffee and Lawrence A. Sherr

4. Faculty Job Satisfaction: Women and Minorities in Peril (924)
   Martha Wingard Tack and Carol Logan Patitu

5. Reconciling Rights and Responsibilities of Colleges and Students: Offensive Speech, Assembly, Drug Testing, and Safety (925)
   Annette Gibbs

6. Creating Distinctiveness: Lessons from Uncommon Colleges and Universities (926)
   Barbara K. Townsend, L. Jackson Newell, and Michael D. Wiese

7. Instituting Enduring Innovations: Achieving Continuity of Change in Higher Education (927)
   Barbara K. Curry

8. Crossing Pedagogical Oceans: International Teaching Assistants in U.S. Undergraduate Education (928)
   Rosslyn M. Smith, Patricia Byrd, Gayle L. Nelson, Ralph Pat Barrett, and Janet C. Constantinides

ORDER FORM 25-8
Quantity **Amount**

_____ Please begin my subscription to the current year's *ASHE-ERIC Higher Education Reports* at $120.00, over 33% off the cover price, starting with Report 1. _____

_____ Please send a complete set of Volume ___ *ASHE-ERIC Higher Education Reports* at $120.00, over 33% off the cover price. _____

Individual reports are available for $24.00 and include the cost of shipping and handling.

SHIPPING POLICY:
- Books are sent UPS Ground or equivalent. For faster delivery, call for charges.
- Alaska, Hawaii, U.S. Territories, and Foreign Countries, please call for shipping information.
- Order will be shipped within 24 hours after receipt of request.
- Orders of 10 or more books, call for shipping information.

All prices shown are subject to change.

Returns: No cash refunds—credit will be applied to future orders.

PLEASE SEND ME THE FOLLOWING REPORTS:

Quantity	Volume/No.	Title	Amount

Please check one of the following:
- ☐ Check enclosed, payable to GW-ERIC.
- ☐ Purchase order attached.
- ☐ Charge my credit card indicated below:
  - ☐ Visa ☐ MasterCard

Expiration Date _____

Subtotal: _____
Less Discount: _____
Total Due: _____

Name _____

Title _____

Institution _____

Address _____

City _____ State _____ Zip _____

Phone _____ Fax _____ Telex _____

Signature _____ Date _____

SEND ALL ORDERS TO: ASHE-ERIC Higher Education Reports
The George Washington University
One Dupont Cir., Ste. 630, Washington, DC 20036-1183
Phone: (202) 296-2597 • Toll-free: (800) 773-ERIC
FAX: (202) 452-1844
URL: www.gwu.edu/~eriche

CALLAHAN LIBRARY
ST. JOSEPH'S COLLEGE
25 Audubon Avenue
Patchogue, NY 11772-2399

LB 3060.3 .O88 1997

Osterlind, Steven J.

A national review of
 scholastic achievement in